RETIREMENT SYSTEMS FOR PUBLIC EMPLOYEES

Pension Research Council

PENSION RESEARCH COUNCIL PUBLICATIONS

The Social Aspects of Retirement—*Otto Pollak*

Positive Experiences in Retirement—*Otto Pollak*

Concepts of Actuarial Soundness in Pension Plans— *Dorrance C. Bronson*

Ensuring Medical Care for the Aged—*Mortimer Spiegelman*

Legal Protection of Private Pension Expectations—*Edwin W. Patterson*

Legal Status of Employee Benefit Rights under Private Pension Plans—*Benjamin Aaron*

Decision and Influence Processes in Private Pension Plans— *James E. McNulty, Jr.*

Fulfilling Pension Expectations—*Dan M. McGill*

Collectively Bargained Multi-Employer Pension Plans—*Joseph J. Melone*

Fundamentals of Private Pensions (Second Edition)—*Dan M. McGill*

Actuarial Aspects of Pension Security—*William F. Marples*

Status of Funding under Private Pension Plans—*Frank L. Griffin, Jr., and Charles L. Trowbridge*

Guaranty Fund for Private Pension Obligations—*Dan M. McGill*

Preservation of Pension Benefit Rights—*Dan M. McGill*

Retirement Systems for Public Employees—*Thomas P. Bleakney*

Retirement Systems for Public Employees

by

THOMAS P. BLEAKNEY, F.S.A.
Consulting Actuary, Milliman and Robertson, Inc.

Published for the

Pension Research Council
Wharton School of the University of Pennsylvania

by

RICHARD D. IRWIN, Inc. *Homewood, Illinois 60430*
IRWIN-DORSEY LIMITED *Georgetown, Ontario L7G 4B3*

First Printing, November 1972
Second Printing, June 1976
Third Printing, August 1976

ISBN 0-256-01407-8
Library of Congress Catalog Card No. 72–90774
Printed in the United States of America

PENSION RESEARCH COUNCIL

PURPOSE OF THE COUNCIL

THE PENSION RESEARCH COUNCIL of the Wharton School of the University of Pennsylvania was created in 1952 for the purpose of sponsoring objective research in the area of private pensions. It was formed in response to the urgent need for a better understanding of the private pension movement. Private pensions have experienced a phenomenal growth during the last three decades, but their economic, political, and social implications are yet to be explored. They seem destined to play a major role in the quest for old-age economic security, but the nature of that role can be ascertained only on the basis of more enlightened evaluation of the capabilities and limitations of the private pension mechanism. It was to conduct an impartial study into the facts and basic issues surrounding private pensions, under the auspices of an academic and professional group representing leadership in every phase of the field, that the Council was organized.

Projects undertaken by the Council are broad in scope and predominantly interpretive rather than technical in nature. In general, attention is concentrated on areas which are not the object of special investigation by other research groups. Its research studies are conducted by mature scholars drawn from both the academic and business spheres. Research results are published from time to time in a series of books and monographs.

FOREWORD

THIS IS the fifteenth publication of the Pension Research Council. It represents the culmination of an effort initiated almost ten years ago. Recognizing the importance of public employee retirement systems in the total economic security structure and keenly aware of some major deficiencies in their design and operation, the Council commissioned a study of this sector of the pension field in 1959. Several abortive attempts were made to get the study under way, but it was not until Thomas Bleakney was persuaded, three years ago, to undertake the task that the study began to move forward. Mr. Bleakney carried out the study in the face of formidable obstacles, with little respite from the heavy professional and administrative burdens associated with his full-time position with a nationally active employee benefit consulting firm.

This study was essentially conceptual in nature, not designed to present a detailed quantitative profile of public employee retirement systems as they exist today in the United States and Canada. Mr. Bleakney examined with a critical eye the environment in which public employee retirement systems operate and called attention to the prevailing concepts, practices, and influences that will have a material bearing on how these plans will fulfill their assigned mission and at what cost to the taxpayers. He points to many inadequacies and anomalies that will have to be corrected before these retirement systems can be considered sound from the standpoint of either the participants or general public policy. He calls especial attention to the urgency of recognizing the accruing cost of pension and other benefits under public employee plans and the adoption of realistic fiscal policies to meet the obligations created by these plans. The book was written at a level and with a focus designed to further the understanding of public employee retirement systems by legislators and others responsible for their proper functioning.

A native of the state of Washington, Mr. Bleakney attended the University of Washington, where he received his Bachelor of Science degree with a major in mathematics and statistics. Following graduation he was employed briefly in the group department of California-Western States Life Insurance Company while awaiting induction into the military service. Upon release from the service, he joined the group department of New York Life Insurance Company. In 1955 he returned to Seattle to join the consulting actuarial staff of Stuart Robertson. Shortly thereafter, when Wendell Milliman left New York Life to form the Milliman and Robertson actuarial consulting firm, Mr. Bleakney accepted an invitation to cast his lot with the new organization. He has been a principal in the firm from its inception. While he serves a wide variety of clients, his activities in recent years have been predominantly in the area of public employee retirement systems. He is a Fellow of the Society of Actuaries, the Canadian Institute of Actuaries, and the Conference of Actuaries in Public Practice, and a member of the American Academy of Actuaries.

The Council is very much indebted to Mr. Bleakney for having taken on this burdensome assignment and seeing it through to a successful completion. He did so at substantial financial and personal sacrifice. The Council is also grateful to Milliman and Robertson, Inc. for having made Mr. Bleakney's services available and to the various members of the firm who lent technical assistance and moral support to Mr. Bleakney. Special acknowledgment is due Wendell Milliman for his unique contribution.

As with any other Council publication, the views and opinions expressed in the book are those of the author and are not necessarily shared by all members of the Council.

Dan M. McGill
October 1972   Research Director

PREFACE

IT WOULD BE unrealistic to expect an author to urge anything but the complete devouring of his creation by its readers. It would be equally unrealistic for any author of a work of this sort to expect any but the most devout students of the subject to do this. As a guide for the vast majority, therefore, particularly those who have legislative or administrative responsibilities for public employee retirement systems, I would urge the reading of the prologue, Chapters 1 and 9, and the introductory remarks in each of the other chapters. In the course of this reading, points of particular interest may come up which can then be pursued in the balance of the text.

At the end of Chapter 1 is a guide to the plan of the book. In brief, the plan is as follows:

Prologue and Chapter 1	Introduction
Chapters 2, 3, and 4	System structure and benefits
Chapters 5 and 6	Financing
Chapter 7	Investments
Chapter 8	Administration
Chapter 9	Summation of matters at issue

The debt I owe to my colleague, Wendell Milliman, for his assistance in this work can never be repaid. In the first place, it was through him that the Pension Research Council provided me with the opportunity (for which, in the more discouraging moments of this work's birth, I have read "inflicted the burden") of discoursing on a subject I find so fascinating. Wendell Milliman reviewed and red-penciled every page of the original draft, and his discussions of many of the more obscure concepts helped immeasurably. His aid was especially valuable for the chapters about financing, in reducing to manageable size and logical order the complex matters discussed.

I am also most grateful for the extensive and detailed suggestions given me by members of the Pension Research Council in their review of drafts of the text. Dr. Dan M. McGill, the Council's research director, had the least enviable task with respect to that review—that of directing my efforts toward a new organization of the material of an earlier draft. He did this with the utmost tact and patience. His guidance and encouragement will always be appreciated.

In distributing my thanks for support in this book's preparation, I certainly must include my staff associates, who did a great deal of the legwork and gathered voluminous statistics, many of which were edited out in the final revisions. Among this group of individuals, particular thanks are due to Charles E. Dean, Jr., who reviewed the entire text and suggested many changes to improve the presentation.

A special place in my acknowledgments is reserved for my secretaries, Tamara Tanner and Leah Woodruff, who, I am sure, despaired of ever seeing the end of the countless redrafts inflicted upon them in my inimitable scrawl.

Finally, a general note of thanks should be extended to all of the others who reviewed the text and gave their suggestions. Space does not permit listing them for individual remarks and appreciation, but it should be noted that I am grateful for their help.

October 1972   THOMAS P. BLEAKNEY

CONTENTS

LIST OF TABLES

Prologue

The Legislative Process

A LEGISLATURE has been compared to the board of directors of a corporation. Legislators have the responsibility of determining government policy but have a minimum of specific administrative duties to perform. This prologue is an attempt to put into focus that portion of a legislator's responsibilities which deals with retirement systems for public employees in his state or province. Many jurisdictions also have legislation affecting retirement plans of private firms, but this function of the legislator is outside the scope of this book.

Consider a hypothetical situation in which a legislator is serving on a committee having before it a bill to increase the benefits to be paid by the public employee retirement system of his state. Assume this system is structured like many others throughout the country. All employees of the state government, other than judges and state police, are members of the system, since membership is required by law. The system also has machinery by which political subdivisions of the state, such as cities and counties, can join. Most such subdivisions have done so. By this action, all of their employees other than teachers, policemen, or firefighters have automatically become members of the system. The excluded employees are earning retirement benefits under separate programs.

The state's public employee retirement system is empowered by law to have the employing agency deduct 5 percent of each employee's monthly salary. This money is invested by the system and either repaid with interest to the member when he terminates employment prior to retirement, or converted to monthly benefits if he remains in the system until retirement. Money is also allocated to the system from each agency of the state government to pay for benefits for its employees, and each political subdivision which has joined the system is similarly assessed its share.

The monthly retirement allowance to be paid to a member who has fulfilled the necessary age and service requirements is made up of two parts. One part is the member's annuity. This is a monthly payment of the actuarial equivalent of all of the contributions which have been deducted from the employee's salary by the system, together with accumulated interest on those deductions as credited by the system from income on its investments. Since the annuity is a repayment of the employee's own money, relatively little legislation affects it.

The balance of the monthly retirement allowance is called the pension. The pension is determined by a formula specified in the governing law. Currently, the monthly pension is calculated as 1 percent of the average salary of the member during his last five years of employment, multiplied by the total number of years of his membership in the system. An additional pension is provided for service with the state or political subdivision prior to the system's establishment.

The legislative committee has before it a proposal to provide a minimum pension benefit. The bill would guarantee each member retiring in the future $10 per month in pension for each year of his membership in the system. The retirement allowance for a person retiring after 30 years of service would thus be at least $300 per month, plus the monthly annuity purchased by his own contribution.

What criteria should the legislator use in evaluating this proposal? The representatives of the employee association have made strong arguments in the bill's favor. They have cited examples of low-salaried members who have retired after several years of service and whose retirement allowances are so inadequate that they are drawing old age assistance checks. They have presented a brief indicating that the total additional benefits to be paid in the next year if the proposal is adopted would be very small. In fact, they show the expenditure to be less than the excess of the current yield on the system's investments over that required to credit interest on accumulated employee contributions and on the reserves developed from employer contributions.

The representative of the retirement system, however, has produced a less favorable report.[1] He agrees with the social merits of having an increase in benefits among the lower income members. He feels that the change in the benefit structure would make the system all the more valuable to its membership and to the political subdivisions who have joined and perhaps to some who are considering joining. On the other hand, he states that the cost is higher than that given by the employees' association representative, and indicates that an increase in the employer contributions to 7 percent of salary from its present 6 percent would be required, if the proposal were adopted. This latter point strikes home to our legislator, since the cost of the employees' salaries and fringe benefits is a major burden on the budget of the state. An increase of 1 percent of salary would require the juggling of priorities of other projects dependent upon the total pool of tax revenue. Accordingly, our legislator must satisfy himself as to the value of the proposal and then measure its effect on the budget.

How can he reconcile the apparently contradictory statements of the employees' and the system's representatives? It is in this area—the measurement of cost—that innumerable misunderstandings arise in retirement programs. This confusion

---

1 Comment by Howard Young, member of the Council: "Here (and elsewhere) it is implied that legislators should be particularly wary of actions advocated by employees or their representatives, and should more often rely on views of representatives of the retirement system. However, it is correctly stated, at the beginning of Chapter 3, that the sole purpose of the system is to provide benefits. Thus legislators, as representatives of both the employees and the employer, must fairly evaluate the interests of both in order to adopt a satisfactory retirement system."

is magnified when benefit proposals became a matter of legislative action.

To attempt to clarify the costing question, it is necessary to differentiate between current out-of-pocket expenditures and accruing costs. The difference is similar to that between cash and accrual bases of accounting, except that "accrual accounting" for a pension plan can result in results overwhelmingly different from those produced by cash accounting.

The employees' representative referred to the additional *cash* expenditures to be made in the next year because of the proposal. These payments would result only from larger benefits to be paid to persons retiring in that year. Ignored was the additional cost for payments in subsequent years, both for the persons now retiring and for those retiring in later years.

The system's figures, on the other hand, may have been determined in a variety of ways. However obtained, they would result in the generation of funds in excess of those required to meet the current disbursements. A build-up of the assets of the fund would thus result from the change. These additional assets would be allocated to those currently active members who will ultimately receive the minimum benefit. The excess funds would thus be disbursed at the time the members' allowances are paid.

The distinction between the two methods of looking at the additional pension cost may be sharpened by drawing a parallel between this problem and another problem facing the legislator. His state is in need of a large new multimillion dollar office building. The use of this building will result in a reduction in the outlay for rents for presently leased quarters. The money required to build the building will be expended over a period of one or two years. Rather than charge the entire cost of this building to the budget of that short period, however, the state will borrow the cost of the building. Annual interest charges and bond retirement payments will spread the cost over the period during which the building will be used.

The analogous situation in a pension plan works in reverse: The time of payment of the pension to an employee comes *after* the use of his services, but the principle involved is similar. If the building is to be paid for by the generation of taxpayers who presumably gain utility from its existence, so also should the pension of a public employee be paid for by the generation of taxpayers who use his services.

A fundamental consideration of the legislator, getting back to the specific problems facing him, should be the *annual accruing cost* of the proposal (estimated at 1 percent of salary), even though the bulk of the *actual expenditure* for the benefits covered in the proposal will be deferred many years.[2] If our legislator is satisfied that he has put a proper price tag on the proposal, he is then prepared to exercise his judgment in balancing the merits of the proposal with its cost. As with so many issues facing him, however, the merits of the proposal are often clouded with many ramifications, some obvious and some not so obvious. Take, for example, the argument made relative to this proposal that it has substantial social benefits in reducing the welfare load by providing a livable pension benefit. A counterargument to this contention is that the state should separate its role as an employer from its role as a welfare agent. If the benefit formula provides a fair benefit for all retirees under the plan, yet produces an inadequate pension because of inadequate pay, such as might generally occur for part-time workers, should not the remedy be charged against the welfare agency of the state rather than against the state and its subdivisions as employers? Further, many persons retired from part-time or short-time public service may have separate pensions or other resources in such amount that a boost in the public pension is unneeded. By this argument, a minimum pension cannot be justified from a welfare standpoint, since the amount of relief payable can only be determined on an individual basis.

One outside benefit which must be reckoned with is the federal old-age benefit, often known as social security. In those jurisdictions where federal old-age benefits are not

---

[2] Chapters 5 and 6 are devoted to a further discussion of the question of funding, including the points of view of those preferring to measure all costs on a cash basis rather than on an accrual basis.

available, there is a tendency for the local retirement systems to have more generous benefit structures than are available where federal benefits are also provided.

All of this leads our legislator to a comparison of his own system with similar systems throughout the country. Evolving as they have over many decades and being subject to differing legislative pressures, the systems vary widely in the benefits they offer. Our legislator may find it difficult to determine where his system stands relative to others. Nevertheless, a review with a broad-brush comparison of his own system's benefit structure to those of other systems will be a necessity for the conscientious legislator. He may also wish to look at the benefits of some typical private employer retirement programs. In comparing the benefits of private and public programs, he must, of course, be aware of the fundamental differences between retirement plans in the public and private sectors. As an example, nearly all public employee retirement systems require employee contributions while relatively few private employees in the United States contribute under their pension plans.

As in so many areas with which the legislator deals, a considerable amount of judgment will be required in evaluating the proposal. Certainly the comparison of his state's system with similar systems is one where sound analysis is greatly needed in determining the equitable level of benefits of his own system.[3]

Our legislator may also recognize some of the more subtle ramifications of the proposal. For example, he will have a personal interest in the change in benefit structure if members of the legislature are covered by the state retirement system. A minimum benefit, in particular, is often of significant importance to legislators, due to the prevalence of salary levels generally lower than those of the average fulltime employee.

Another subtle consideration the legislator must keep in

---

[3] Chapters 2, 3, and 4 deal in some depth with the questions of benefit structure and should be referred to by the reader interested in pursuing this facet more thoroughly.

mind is the "leapfrogging" effect this proposed change might have on those public employees in the state who are not covered by this system. For example, if the teachers are covered by a system not presently having a minimum benefit, will this proposed change lead to a similar request from the teachers? If so, what will be the cost of such a proposal? Will the arguments supplied for the present proposal apply equally well to the teachers? Is there an alternate form of benefit which the teachers have which has similar provisions, but is not precisely the same as the current proposal? If so, would the alternate form be acceptable to the persons proposing the present change, and what would be its cost? Although these questions might not immediately come forth as explicitly, the applicable ones should enter into the mind of the legislator, anticipating future proposals of the teachers which might add expense to the teachers' system and bring about counterproposals for balancing increases in the public employee system.

Still another consideration for our legislator might be the follow-up proposal which is likely to be before some subsequent session of his legislature, extending the minimum benefit to presently retired members. If the current proposal has a companion piece of legislation, either at the present time or logically succeeding it, the companion's cost should be recognized and the likelihood of its becoming law measured.

In the legislator's state, as in many, the "ratchet effect" bears upon any decision made relative to public employee systems. By law or legal precedent, a formula for pension benefits once granted to a specific employee cannot be reduced. A pension plan's commitment may extend in a few cases for nearly 100 years, from the point of employment to the death of the last survivor deriving benefits from the employee's membership in the system. If any program or modification should be so poorly designed as to create intolerable costs, the ratchet effect would allow corrective action only with respect to employees hired after the new enactment. The legislature would be powerless to cure the problem for current employees. This places a heavy burden upon the legislature to make a well-considered initial decision in all pension legislation.

Unfortunately, this burden is not always carried properly, and, in particular, appropriate emphasis is not always placed upon the cost of proposed benefits. The deficiency arises either because the legislature does not require satisfactory reports regarding additional costs, or because of the use of pay-as-you-go funding methods, where the true costs of proposed benefits will not be felt for many years. Because of the pressures that arise in the course of a legislative session, it is easy to call for a pleasant tune when the piper is not to be paid until the meeting of a subsequent legislature.

Even greater irresponsibility is bred where the legislature sets the benefit level for the state's political subdivisions but is not itself required to meet the budgets of these political subdivisions. The fiscal problems of our cities are widespread and widely known, yet in many states and provinces the legislatures can and do aggravate these problems by increasing the required benefits for municipal employees, particularly policemen and firefighters, without making available to the municipalities corresponding sources of revenue.

In this regard, it must be recognized that analyses of the logic of the various arguments will not be made in a political vacuum, desirable as that might sometimes be. Instead, our legislator will be subject to pressures of various sorts from the parties directly or indirectly interested in the proposal. The arguments brought forth by the lobbyists might well be quite objective and help him crystallize his own thinking on the issue. Nevertheless, a rare phenomenon will be the person who can cast his vote oblivious to all political considerations. Such a person may also find on occasion that he will not be around to vote on similar questions in future legislatures.

This book is devoted to an analysis of various aspects of public retirement systems. Although it is not specifically concerned with the legislative procedure as such, no study of retirement systems in the public sector can ignore the legislative process. While a private retirement plan can be the creation of an individual, the public plan is perforce the product of legislative enactment and often of compromise. The effect of practical politics on the results should always be in view.

Chapter 1

An Overview

As a practical matter, the provision for an employee's non-productive years is a joint responsibility of the individual, his employer, and the government. Whether for good or ill, an increasing share of this responsibility is being borne by the government (through social security programs) and by employers (by means of formal retirement systems). This book is concerned with the problems of retirement systems established by governmental bodies in their roles as employers.

The term *public employee retirement system* is widely used throughout this book. The term refers to a state, provincial, or local retirement system covering public employees in the United States or Canada. Not included are the retirement systems for civilian and military employees of the federal governments of the United States and Canada. Also excluded are the federal programs of old-age benefits under social security,[1] although the effects of these programs on benefit design and cost are discussed.

---

[1] The term *social security* will be used to refer to these programs in each country, even though this usage of the phrase has not received the same broad acceptance in Canada as it has in the United States. The programs encompassed by the term in Canada will be the Old Age Security Plan, the Canada Pension Plan, and the Quebec Pension Plan.

10

The payment of benefits to a retired person or his beneficiary is an outgrowth of the employment relationship. The cost of providing such benefits may be considered as part of the payment for the services rendered. However, there is a substantial time lag between performance of the services which give rise to the benefits and their payment. The employee who first becomes covered by a retirement program at age 25 may still be receiving retirement income when he is 85 or 90. On the average, there is a 30 to 40 year lag between the service for which retirement income is a reward and the time when retirement benefits are paid.

It is thus apparent that the establishment and management of retirement programs involve long-range considerations. The purpose of this book is to give those who are concerned with public employee retirement systems an understanding of these considerations. The issues involved in the management of these plans will be explored. Hopefully there will be some helpful guidance imparted to those charged with the responsibility of establishing and maintaining these systems.

THE SCOPE OF THE SYSTEMS' COVERAGE

The first public employee retirement system in the United States was established in 1857, covering New York City policemen. The next half century brought other municipal plans into existence, including a number of systems for teachers. It was not until 1911, though, that Massachusetts became the first state to develop a system to cover its general state employees. Since that time membership in public systems has grown until it is now nearly universal among nonfederal employees, covering over 90 percent of state, provincial, and local employees in the United States and Canada.

The systems themselves number approximately 2,300. They range in size from the three largest, whose combined membership exceeds one million, to the majority in number, each of which covers less than 100 employees, a handful having only a single member each. In total, these systems provide benefits for approximately eight million employees and their beneficiaries.

The membership extends over almost the entire gamut of occupations, from accountant to zoologist. Included are nearly all of the teachers at all scholastic levels and most of the continent's judges, firefighters and policemen, as well as the majority of its much-maligned bureaucrats.

The most important benefits these retirement systems provide are awarded to employees who complete the necessary age and service requirements for retirement. Nearly all systems also provide death and disability benefits, both for injury on the job and sickness or injury off the job. The death benefits take many forms, including continuation of retirement benefits to a survivor after the death of a retired employee or a pension or cash benefit to a survivor upon the death of an active employee.

While benefits can be provided without the formality of a written document, this is neither practical nor advisable for large employers and may not be legally possible for governmental bodies in the United States and Canada. Written provisions help to assure uniform treatment for all employees and to facilitate orderly retirement as the employees complete their working years. A well-conceived program of benefits will enable retired employees to live in reasonable security. It will also serve as an instrument for attracting new employees and retaining existing employees.

The written provisions of a public employee retirement system may either take the form of law, as is common for the large systems, or be embodied in a formal plan document similar to those used for the same purpose in the private sector. However constituted, the system's governing provisions will define:

1. Who is eligible and how those who are eligible become members of the system;
2. What benefits accrue and the conditions governing their payment;

3. How the costs of the system will be shared between employer and employee.

CONTROL OF PUBLIC SYSTEMS

There is a significant difference between public and private retirement programs with respect to the decision-making process. A private company's self-interest is best served if proposals for the establishment or change of a retirement plan for the company are evaluated by competent actuaries and reviewed by the company's financial officers before action is taken. If the plan is subject to collective bargaining, the cost of each improvement in benefits is recognized as a part of the package of payroll costs. In well-managed companies, any action to increase or modify retirement benefits is made with full knowledge of resulting cost implications.

In contrast, the level or kind of benefits to be provided in public employee retirement systems and the financing of those benefits are subject to decisions made under pressure in a political atmosphere. Ideally, orderly procedures should exist to assure that the cost implications of liberalization of eligibility provisions and benefit levels are evaluated before the legislators are asked to take action. Rarely do such procedures exist, and even where they do, they frequently work imperfectly. The result is that all too often the problem of financing new or improved benefits under public employee retirement systems is not confronted until after the employer is firmly committed to the increased benefits.

A new element has been introduced in recent years as public employees have won or enlarged the right to bargain collectively. Changes in eligibility or benefit provisions in retirement systems have thus become the subjects of negotiations between representatives of employee groups and their employers at the state, provincial, or local level. Deep conflicts may arise if an agreement reached by such a negotiation fails to be ratified by the legislative authority governing the system. The problem is especially acute if the negotiation is with a local governmental body but the required amending legislation is at the state or provincial level.

THE NEED TO KNOW COSTS

By the very nature of pension obligations there is a time lag between the accruing of pension rights and the payment of benefits. If funds are set aside and invested at the time pension rights accrue, part of the money necessary to meet the benefit payments can be provided from the resulting investment income. There are strong arguments for funding the costs of retirement benefits during the period of services upon which the employee's benefits are founded. Despite these arguments, however, some political entities, either as a matter of policy or as a result of budgetary pressures, elect either to do no funding or to provide only partial funding of pension benefits.

Whatever the policy in this regard, if a legislative body is to operate in a financially responsible manner in reviewing a proposal to modify a public employee retirement system, it must be adequately informed as to the proposal's expected costs. These costs may be presented either in terms of the expected incidence of benefit payments over a number of years or as the amount required to meet the cost of the benefits as they are being earned. In either event, the calculations should be performed by a qualified actuary[2] who is trained to make such evaluations competently.

Presentation of data of this sort will keep the legislature fully advised in advance of the cost implications of any change which it might make in a public employee retirement system. One important reason for the legislature's being so advised is that the provisions of many retirement systems for public employees are viewed by the courts as having the status of employment contracts. This view prevents the provisions from subsequently being modified to the detriment of

---

[2] Laws or regulations in many states permit services of this type to be performed only by qualified actuaries. Definitions of a "qualified actuary" often include membership in the American Academy of Actuaries.

any employee covered by it at the time of change. Thus a legislature cannot recant on the granting of overly expensive improvements in benefits.

THE FUNDING QUESTION

As already indicated, a policy which assures that the legislators are aware of the cost implications of proposed pension plan changes before acting upon them does not necessarily govern the actual monetary commitments for the resulting costs. Regardless of the financing method adopted, the ultimate outlay will be dependent upon the actual benefit payments made, increased by the administrative expenses incurred, and decreased by the investment income earned upon any accumulated funds. Except for any differences in investment earnings resulting from differences in the size of the funds, the ultimate costs, then, will be the same, whatever financing method is adopted. Why, then, fund pension costs in advance?

A strong case can be made for the proposition that retirement benefits constitute a form of deferred, contingent, additional compensation for the services of the employee. If this proposition is accepted, then the cost of such compensation must be regarded as an expense to be recognized at the time the services are performed. If the conditions of the retirement program are met by an employee (i.e., if he remains in employment for the necessary period of time, makes any necessary contributions, and survives to the time of eligibility for benefit payments), then he is entitled to the utmost assurance that he will be paid the additional compensation to which he is entitled as a result of his service for the employer. Meeting of the costs of retirement benefits as those benefits are earned will create a fund which the employee can look to for such assurance.

Another argument for meeting the costs of pension benefits as services are performed is that the investment income earned on the funds thereby developed can substantially reduce the employer's ultimate payment for such benefits.

Finally, although it may be difficult or distasteful to raise taxes or defer other desired projects in order to fund pension costs on a current basis, there is little reason to believe that such alternatives will be less burdensome in the future.

Some or all of these propositions have been disputed. Some persons contend that pension costs constitute a gratuity and are not a form of deferred compensation. Indeed, one court has stated that pension benefits for governmental employees are in the "nature of a bounty springing from the appreciation and graciousness of the sovereign."[3]

Others, while accepting the additional compensation concept, do not concede that this logically requires that the expense of such additional compensation be met while the services are being performed. With respect to the need for security,[4] it is contended that the taxing power of the state provides adequate security. It is also contended that it is uneconomic for a political body to borrow money, on the one hand, to finance expenditures and thereby incur an obligation to pay interest, while setting aside current tax revenues, on the other hand, to be invested and earn interest to meet future retirement system disbursements.

While the author finds the arguments in favor of advance funding more persuasive than the contrary ones, the reader is left to make his own choice. One of the contrary arguments occasionally offered is the example of the federal old-age benefit systems of the United States and Canada, which are financed on substantially a pay-as-you-go basis in practice. Comparing the financing of such systems with the financing of public employee retirement systems is hardly to the point. A federal old-age benefit system is essentially one under which, for social objectives, a portion of the nation's goods is transferred between the working population and those who

---

3 *Blough* v. *Ekstrom,* 14 Ill, App. 2nd 153, 160, 144 N. E. 2nd 436, 440 (2nd Dist. 1957) .

4 In Canada, where a substantial percentage of the securities held by public employee retirement systems is in provincial and local bonds (see Table 5, p. 138) , this argument can be extended to contend that an employer's unfunded system is as secure as one invested solely in the bonds of the employer.

are no longer in the working population. Furthermore, because the federal government can create money through its fiscal policies, allocating a portion of the money created by the issuance of federal securities to the old-age fund is no different than omitting the entire exercise.

PLAN OF THE BOOK

The foregoing remarks give an outline of the environment of public employee retirement systems today. These matters and others will be discussed in the remainder of this book.

The next three chapters are concerned with the structure of retirement systems—the scope of their coverage, the makeup of their membership, and the benefits they provide. The two succeeding chapters, Chapters 5 and 6, deal with the questions of financing the systems from the two aspects of determining the magnitude of accruing costs and the meeting of those costs. Chapter 7 covers a related topic, the investment of the funds developed by the systems. A discussion of the administrative matters with which each system must be concerned is given in Chapter 8. The final chapter is devoted to an evaluation of the issues raised in the book.

Chapter 2

The Systems and Their Membership

RETIREMENT BENEFITS for public employees are generally provided through the vehicle of a formal retirement system. The system may be a unit of government with its own statutorily established controlling board or officer and administrative staff, or it may be merely a framework of laws and regulations, with no status as an agency or department. However it is constituted, participation in the benefits it provides is often referred to as *membership* in the system. This chapter discusses the foundations of such membership— the systems themselves, the persons eligible to join, and the financial commitments of the members.

RETIREMENT SYSTEMS

Many states and provinces have two large public employee retirement systems and a number of smaller ones. One of the large systems provides benefits for teachers through the twelfth grade level, sometimes including junior college staff, but generally excluding academic employees at the four-year college level. The other large system is for all other employees of the state or province itself, excluding any employees who might be included in small, specialized systems, such as those for the highway patrol or judges. Political subdivisions, such as the counties, municipalities, and water districts, are often eligible to join the state employees' system, making the system's benefits available to the local employees. Some local units may set up independent systems for their policemen, firefighters, or other employees. All told, a typical state or province might have 50 systems, many with their own controlling boards or committees, investment programs, and administrative personnel and equipment. Although some systems have common benefits imposed by state or provincial laws, such as systems for policemen and firefighters, many have selected their own benefit patterns, leading to a multiplicity of benefit structures.

While many states[1] come close to the pattern just described, there are also many variations. Some states have one large system covering all state employees and teachers and, on an optional basis, the employees of political subdivisions. Some states have statewide systems for policemen, or firefighters, or both. Some states provide a separate system from the state system for employees of political subdivisions. Many states provide coverage for their college and university professional staff with the Teachers Insurance and Annuity Association, a nonprofit insurance company which serves in many ways as a federal system for these employees.

Although there are many public employee retirement systems in existence, most covered employees are members of relatively large systems. For example, approximately half of the provincial, state, and local employees covered by retirement plans in the United States and Canada hold membership in systems of more than 50,000 members. Nearly 90 percent are in systems having at least 10,000 members. These large systems are generally administered at the state level for teachers, state employees, employees (other than teachers) of those political subdivisions which have elected to join the systems, or for combinations of these. Nearly all of the large

---

[1] The term "state" is used to encompass state or province, unless specifically noted to the contrary.

systems deal with more than one governmental unit; the term *conglomerate* will be used to describe such a system. This multiemployer characteristic distinguishes most large systems from the small systems, which are often administered by a single city, county, or other governmental unit.

Advantages of Conglomeration. There has been an increasing tendency for the conglomerate systems to grow and the smaller systems to be eliminated. This can have many salutary results to the taxpayer and to members:

Consolidation of administration with resulting reduced expense.

Better investment results because of the ability to afford investment counsel and because of greater diversification.

Spreading of the risk of adverse mortality experience.

Elimination of competition between systems for increasing benefits and consequent *leapfrogging,* where systems take turns catching and passing each other in benefits.

Elimination of the forfeiture or reduction of benefits for employees who change public employers within the system.[2]

Improved services to members because of a larger professional staff.

Sounder benefit design because of the legislature's freedom to limit its attention to a few systems.

A corollary to the last advantage listed above is that conglomeration imposes the full responsibility for a system's well-being upon the legislature. In contrast, some legislatures require cities and political subdivisions to set up their own systems and provide specified levels of benefits. Where this occurs, responsibility for proper financing of the benefits is often lacking. The legislature passes the job to the cities. The cities, especially those with already strained budgets, may do little to meet the costs of the programs but wait instead for the legislature to bail them out when the financing of prob-

---

2 See p. 70.

lems become critical. Such a division of responsibility may thus mean no responsibility. This problem can be avoided by adopting a statewide program, leaving the legislature with full control of both benefits and financing.

Division of responsibility between the state and its political subdivisions can have another effect. By using a two-front attack, employees may exact benefit liberalizations which would otherwise be denied. The first appeal is to the local employers. Failing in this, the employees can go over the employers' heads to the legislature. Political considerations might override the employers' objections, regardless of their validity, and cause the legislature to require the payment of the improved benefits.

Disadvantages of Conglomeration. Favorable results do not necessarily attend all conglomerations. The arguments against conglomeration are those offered against any large organization—concentration of political power, the inertia of a bureaucratic administrative staff, and inflexibility. The last characteristic, inflexibility, applies not only to administration, where a large system must enforce rules which cannot fit all situations equally well, but also to the area of benefit structure. In a small system, the employer has the freedom to custom-design the plan of benefits to reflect the needs of the community. An example of the value of this right might occur in a retirement community drawing a significant portion of its employees from older persons who have retired from other occupations. A conventional benefit structure for such employees might prove both unduly expensive and inappropriate in the level of benefits provided.

As the fund amassed by a conglomerate system becomes very large, another disadvantage of conglomeration emerges. Managing the investments of a very large fund presents unique problems. Large blocks of securities are not easily bought or sold. Thus the large funds cannot be as agile in their security trading as the smaller funds. A survey of 634 private pension plans showed that among the majority whose funds are valued at market, those having assets between $25 million and $50 million fared substantially better in annual yield (5.3 percent) than those over $200 million (3.4 percent) during the 1965–1969 period.[3] Some large systems meet this problem by splitting their funds and investing the separate portions independently, often with independent money managers.

Inflexibility in a multiagency system can lead to a more subtle defect. This is best categorized by the word *antiselection,* an insurance term referring to the acquisition of insurance covering a worse-than-average risk with the expectation of financial gain at the expense of the insurer. A form of antiselection occurs where a unit participates in a public employee retirement system in order to provide its employees retirement benefits which are expected to cost more than the contributions of the unit and its members. Opportunities for such antiselection are great if all employers participating in a system pay the same percentage of salary, regardless of their inherent pension costs. Dramatic examples of antiselection have occurred in systems providing benefits related to the salary of each employee in his last year or two of employment. By raising employees' salaries shortly before their retirement, employers have increased those employees' retirement benefits out of proportion to the contributions which have been made to the system over the employees' working careers. Obviously this type of abuse can occur in most systems. In a system covering only one political unit, however, the unit will ultimately pay the price for this practice and may be motivated to avoid it. In a conglomerate system, if the practice occurs rarely, the cost will be spread over all employers, and no incentive is given the offending employer to refrain from the abuse.[4]

Political Conclusions. Regardless of the theoretical conclusions which might emerge from a balancing of the advantages and disadvantages, efforts to consolidate retirement

---

[3] *First Annual McGraw-Hill/Standard & Poor's/Intercapital Inc. Pension Fund Management Survey* (New York, 1971), Table VIII. The yields given include all capital gains, both realized and unrealized.

[4] See also p. 41 regarding legislation in New York State resulting from this practice.

systems into larger units may fall by the wayside because of political pressures. One of the greatest deterrents is the common phenomenon of empire building. Combining two or more systems into one results in fewer titles, fewer boards and fewer persons bearing the trappings of office, minimal as they may be. Unless the benefit structure can be improved by the merger, employee groups may object to consolidation due to the dilution of their ability to exert influence on the workings of the larger system. This type of opposition from both the systems' administrative staffs and members may thwart a proposed consolidation of systems, no matter how logical the consolidation might otherwise appear.

QUALIFYING FOR MEMBERSHIP

Mere employment by an employer does not necessarily entitle a person to participate in the employer's retirement system. Part-time, temporary, or seasonal employees may be excluded by statute or regulation. There may be a waiting period before participation in a retirement system can begin. Two or more systems may be provided by an employer for different occupational categories, or there may be a benefit differential by job within a single system. A former employee returning to work may be subject to special provisions. These prerequisites to membership vary between systems and are the subject of the next several subsections.

Employment Status. In many smaller systems, distinguishing eligible employees from those not eligible is quite straightforward. This is particularly true among systems covering policemen and firefighters, where a formal commissioning takes place, clearly defining the employee's status. In other relatively stable positions, such as clerical jobs, defining who is to be included in a system's coverage can also be easy. Problems arise in categorizing an employee who works in a job only needed during the summer, or as a janitor three hours each night, or on a fee basis, rather than as a direct employee. Where the system is small, problem cases such as these can be reviewed individually. If the system is meant to cover only full-time employees, the facts can be ascertained. If there is more than one criterion for membership, a judgment can be rendered in questionable situations. If a case comes up that was not anticipated when the governing rules and regulations were adopted, the rules and regulations may be changed to fit the new situation.

The larger systems, on the other hand, tend to have more formal participation requirements, because of their size and the diverse types of employment they cover. Generally, the rules are designed to grant eligibility only to those employees who work full-time or nearly so. For example, in the California Public Employees' Retirement System, membership is restricted to full-time positions and to half-time (or better) positions extending for more than one year. The administration of requirements of this sort often entails elaborate and detailed rulings to cover the great number of variations that will arise in special work situations.

Age or Service Requirements. A clear majority of public employees are in retirement systems granting immediate participation to employees in covered job classifications when they are hired.[5] In those systems which impose service requirements on the right of an employee to membership, 6 to 12 months must be served in most cases. In rare instances, the employee must also have attained a certain age, such as 30. In some systems, employees hired at advanced ages, such as over 60, are excluded from membership.

A waiting period may be justified on the grounds of administrative economy. One expense that the use of a wait-

---

[5] Social Security Administration Research Reports No. 15 and 23: *State and Local Government Retirement Systems, 1965* and *Retirement Systems for Employees of State and Local Governments, 1966.* Approximately 75 percent of the employees covered in the Social Security Administration surveys were in systems providing immediate participation, regardless of age, in all areas of covered employment. The majority of the rest of the members were in systems having only maximum age restrictions. Less than 10 percent had minimum age or service requirements. A sampling of Canadian systems made by the author showed about 40 percent of the employees were in systems having immediate participation, about 25 percent in systems with only a maximum age restriction, and about 35 percent in systems with a minimum age or service requirement.

ing period avoids is that involved in setting up membership files for employees who terminate after short periods of service. A waiting period also eliminates the need to withhold and record employee contributions which are retained briefly and then returned. The more widely held viewpoint, however, is that there are significant advantages in having an employee begin to participate at the outset of his career. If an employee is covered as he comes on the payroll, any required contributions are deducted from his very first paycheck, causing him to become immediately aware of the cost of his participation in the system. In contrast, when an employee does not join a system until some time after he goes to work, the reduction in his take-home pay because of his required contribution can cause dissatisfaction. At the employer level, administration is simplified when each employee is brought into the system at his hiring date. Enrollment in the system can accompany the other personnel transactions taking place at hire, rather than requiring a special follow-up procedure when the waiting period is completed some time later. Furthermore, if the employer contribution to the system is set as a percentage of covered payroll, immediate participation simplifies the determination of the required aggregate contribution of a department and makes budget estimation easier. The employee also gains by immediate participation because of the increased benefit which results from the additional services credited to him.

Reemployment. Very commonly, an employee who transfers between participating employers maintains his membership in a system as if there were no termination of employment. Similarly, an employee rehired under the same system after a short break in service will retain credit for the service prior to his termination.

A somewhat more complex situation arises when an employee is rehired after an extended break in his covered employment. A common provision allows such an employee to reinstate previous credits by the repayment of any contributions he might have withdrawn. In a system where this is not allowed, an employee may nonetheless have the right to maintain his previously credited service under a vesting provision of the system.[6]

Another type of reemployment occurs among members who have previously retired. Of primary interest here is the effect the reemployment will have on the retirement benefit. This is discussed in the next chapter.[7]

EMPLOYEE CONTRIBUTIONS

Only about one employee out of every four covered by a private retirement plan in the United States is required to help pay for the plan by means of employee contributions.[8] This pattern is markedly different from the general rule among public employees. In fact, over 90 percent of the members of public employee retirement systems are required to make contributions.[9] This difference in practice displays a consistent adherence by most public employee retirement systems[10] to the philosophy that once prevailed in all plans—joint financing of retirement benefits.

Advantages of Contributory Systems.   An early expression of this philosophy was given by the Commission on Pensions of New York City in 1918, as their grounds for recommending the adoption of contributory systems for that city:

---

6 See p. 68.

7 See p. 49.

8 U.S. Department of Labor: Bureau of Labor Statistics, *Labor Mobility and Private Pension Plans,* Bulletin No. 1407, 1964.

9 Of 264 systems providing usable data in response to two surveys of the Social Security Administration in the United States and to the author's survey of Canadian systems, 251 systems were contributory. See Social Security Administration Research Reports No. 15 and 23: *State and Local Government Retirement Systems, 1965* and *Retirement Systems for Employees of State and Local Governments, 1966.*

10 A notable exception is found in the state of New York. Under a 1960 amendment to the governing laws of the New York Public Employees' Retirement System, the state and all participating political subdivisions which have so elected make additional contributions to replace all or a portion of their employees' contributions. This feature of the system, which is referred to in the law as "pensions-for-increased-take-home-pay," has converted the New York system from a fully contributory to a noncontributory system for the majority of its members. In similar fashion, the New York State Teachers' Retirement System and other systems in New York have become largely noncontributory.

A system in which both parties contribute is proposed because . . . of the sense of mutual responsibility thereby fostered for the provision of benefits which will be equitable and advantageous to both parties. . . . Through the responsibilities thereby developed for the provision and retention of benefits equitable to both parties, there would be a natural check on overliberal interpretation and legalized liberalization of the provisions which would make the system unduly costly to either party.[11]

A restatement of this philosophy with a slightly different twist and the advantage of 50 additional years of experience is found in succinct comments made by the Legislative Retirement Study Commission in its report to the 1971 legislative session of the state of Minnesota. Among several other guidelines for the legislature, the Commission includes the following statement of principle:

Governmental employer support of normal level pension costs should not exceed equal matching of the employee's contribution to his pension, except as to certain law enforcement and safety employees. To provide a greater share of the benefits at governmental expense tempts employees to strive for extra benefits and marginal benefits because the cost to the employee is small. Pensions should not become "hidden extra salary."[12]

These statements embrace the concept that the costs of benefit improvements should be shared between the parties. This in turn necessitates cost determinations which will provide a basis for this sharing. Within this framework, a contributory system can provide retirement benefits in an environment of responsible management where the costs are known and shared.[13] It will be noted that this concept is not always conspicuously present. It will also be noted, incidentally, that the goals of responsible management can be met in a noncontributory system if the costs (after having been appropriately

---

11 Commission on Pensions, *Report on the Pension Funds of the City of New York* (New York, 1918), pp. 15–16.

12 Legislative Retirement Study Commission, *Report to the 1971 Legislative Session of the State of Minnesota* (St. Paul, 1971), p. 12.

13 The information needed for the costs to be known will be discussed in Chapter 5.

determined and disclosed) are recognized by both the employer and employees as alternatives to similar expenditures in direct payroll. This approach involves pricing pension costs in cents per hour, an idea that is widely accepted in collective bargaining in the private sector.

From the employee's viewpoint, a strong argument favoring his making contributions is the leverage it gives him in enforcing his rights to benefits and in insisting on adequate employer contributions. The employee who makes his contribution has a moral, if not a legal, right to expect the employer to do likewise. For the same reason, the employee may have stronger cause to believe that the retirement program will be maintained than if he were not making contributions. This concept was stated by President Franklin D. Roosevelt in a reference to the United States social security program:

We put those payroll contributions there so as to give the contributors a legal, moral, and political right to collect their pensions and their unemployment benefits. With those taxes in there, no damn politician can ever scrap my social security program.[14]

Disadvantages of Contributory Systems. Probably the greatest of the disadvantages of contributory systems in the United States is that contributions made by the employee must be paid from after-tax dollars. The employee must include contributions deducted from his salary in his taxable income, even though they are locked into the fund and he does not have use of them while he remains at work. This disadvantage is offset to a slight extent after retirement, when a portion of his pension is tax free. However, this offset is of no value to many retired employees, since it is common for a retired employee's personal exemptions and deductions to exceed his taxable income. The importance of these tax considerations in plan design is difficult to measure. It is interesting to note, however, that in Canada, where salary deductions for contributions to registered pension plans are

---

14 Arthur M. Schlesinger, Jr., *The Coming of the New Deal* (Boston: 1957), p. 308.

tax-deductible, contributory plans are much more common, covering over 60 percent of employees under retirement plans in the private sector.[15]

Contributory plans have other drawbacks besides adverse tax consequences. A contributory plan is more difficult and expensive to administer. Employee contributions are inconsistent with the growing recognition of pensions as deferred compensation, rather than as joint savings programs. A contributory plan may inhibit good employee relations, particularly among those who are many years from retirement. For the younger employee, the required contribution may be looked upon as an onerous burden to be met at a time in his career when he is least able to afford it. Finally, if a given level of employer and employee contributions is set aside under a contributory plan, that same level, contributed solely by the employer, will generally produce greater benefits. This is partially due to savings in expense, but in larger part is due to the avoidance of refunds to employees upon termination of service prior to retirement.[16]

Level of Contributions. Under a contributory system, the employee normally contributes a stated portion of his monthly salary—typically, 4 to 6 percent. This contribution is a form of savings deposit, since eventually it will be returned in the form of retirement, death, or disability benefits, or refunded upon termination of employment. In this respect, public employee retirement systems differ from social security where the contributions are, in effect, taxes levied to provide funds to pay benefits to current beneficiaries. The employee's obligation is usually expressed as a percentage of all, or a part of, his earnings. A fixed-dollar contribution is seldom used. This reflects the correlation between contributions and benefits, since the latter are also nearly always related to salary. The actual amount an employee contributes varies considerably among the different public employee

---

[15] Statistics Canada, *Pension Plans in Canada, 1970* (Ottawa, 1972) .

[16] This cost disadvantage of contributory plans is diminished or eliminated to the extent that employees forfeit vested benefits upon termination of employment in order to collect their accumulated contributions. See p. 69.

retirement systems. This variance is due not only to differences in the contribution rates themselves, but also to differences in the salary bases to which the rates are applied.

The majority of public employee systems express the employee contribution in terms of a percentage, or a range of percentages, of the member's total basic earnings, exclusive of overtime pay or any other special allowances. For the purpose of administering payrolls, this method is probably the most economical and has all the other advantages of simplicity. Nevertheless, a significant number of systems require contributions on earnings up to a specified amount only. Common limits are $3,600, $4,800, $6,000, and $7,500. The lowest two of these limits reflect the United States social security wage bases during different periods. A variation on this pattern occurs in many systems, where contributions are made at a specified rate on annual earnings up to similar dollar limits, and then at a higher rate on all earnings in excess of such limits.

Although typical employee contribution rates might be 4 to 6 percent of earnings, actual contribution rates vary over a much wider range. In a number of systems the employee contribution rates vary by a member's sex, the age at which he enters the plan, and sometimes the type of work he does. The percentages of salary contributed by members of a system of this type are given in Table 1. The reasons for the variation in contributions by age and sex in this table are

TABLE 1
Employee Contribution Rates,
New Jersey Public Employees'
Retirement System

Age at Entry	Percentage of Salary	
	Male	*Female*
25	4.91	5.51
30	5.19	5.85
35	5.59	6.30
40	6.04	6.81
45	6.55	7.39
50	7.12	8.02
55	7.84	8.83

related to the benefits provided under the system.[17] In most of the systems with this type of contribution schedule, member contributions, accumulated to retirement, are designed to provide a specified portion (often one half) of the total retirement benefit.

Interest Credited on Employee Contributions. In the type of system just mentioned, where there is a direct relationship between the accumulated employee contributions and the retirement benefit, vital issues are involved in determining the rate of crediting interest on the accumulated contributions and the rate basis used for converting these accumulated contributions into annuities at retirement.[18] Extended litigation involving these issues has occurred in some systems, an indication of the importance of proper treatment of employee contributions in public employee retirement systems.

An important consideration in determining the rate of interest to be credited in accumulating employee contributions is whether employee contributions are to be viewed as savings of the employee or as part of his price for the retirement benefit. The employee who terminates before retirement has made his contributions as a form of forced savings. While the same might be said for the employee who remains in employment until he retires, his savings then serve the primary purpose of providing a contribution towards the total cost of his retirement benefit.

It is significant, in this regard, that employee contributions in public employee retirement systems are nearly always a condition of employment: All new employees must join the system and make the required contributions when they become eligible. If employee contributions are regarded as a form of forced savings, an employee might well contend in equity that his contributions should be credited with interest at a rate comparable to that which they would receive in an equally safe investment of his own choosing.

---

17 See p. 39.

18 See p. 41 regarding annuity conversion rates.

In practice, a wide spectrum of philosophies appear to exist in the crediting of interest on employee contributions. At one extreme are systems where an employee is not only paid no interest but forfeits all of his contributions if he should terminate early in his career. This type of provision, where it exists, is usually found in a system covering policemen or firefighters.

Not quite so adverse to the employee, but confiscatory nonetheless, are systems which credit no interest on the contributions of terminating employees. There are also systems which pay only a nominal rate of interest, such as 2 or 3 percent, on the accumulated contributions. In these systems, the employee who terminates is, in effect, making a contribution towards the pension of his fellow workers, in the amount of the foregone additional interest on his contributions.

Many systems, particularly the larger ones, credit interest on the accumulated contributions of each member at a rate approximately equal to the earnings rate of the system as a whole. This technique puts the employee in an equitable position with the employer as to the earnings on the funds contributed by the respective parties. In a well-managed system, the interest so credited will compare favorably with that provided by other savings media, such as banks, savings bonds, and life insurance.

Chapter 3

Normal Retirement Benefits

A RETIREMENT SYSTEM exists solely for the purpose of providing benefits. A system's array of benefits may be referred to collectively as its benefit structure. The foundation of that structure is the benefit provided to members of the system when their working careers are completed. Such benefits—the normal retirement benefits—are the subject of this chapter. The next chapter will deal with other types of benefits provided by public employee retirement systems.

In a few plans, everyone who qualifies for normal retirement receives the same benefit amount. However, in order to produce a more equitable pension, most plans use benefit formulas which vary the pension at retirement with the amount of service credited to the retiring employee and with his level of compensation. In some plans a maximum level of benefits is reached by a person who retires after a specified number of years of service, and a proportionately reduced benefit is provided for employees retiring with less service. The same effect is achieved in other plans by accruing units of benefit for each year of credited service up to a specified maximum. In many plans no maximum exists and additional benefit units accrue as long as the employee works.

TYPES OF BENEFIT FORMULAS

One of the earliest public employee retirement systems in the United States was the New York State Employees' System. The benefit structure used by that system at its establishment was followed by many other public employee retirement systems in the United States. The philosophy underlying that structure was summarized in a report of the Commission on Pensions of the State of New York in 1920:

> The cost of the system should be concurrently shared by State and employees. . . . Employees should make contributions . . . computed to be adequate to provide approximately one half the service benefit, and . . . the other half of the service benefit should be provided by the State. The . . . contributions of each employee should be held for the sole use of the contributing employee. . . . At retirement, the employee should receive the actuarial equivalent of the contributions made.[1]

Later in the report these general statements were converted to specifics, which still govern some of the contributing members of the system:

> The retirement allowance granted upon service retirement consists of the pension granted by the State and an annuity provided by the contributions of the employee. The pension and annuity are approximately equal in most cases, and together provide for the average employee a total allowance of about half the final compensation

1. Allowed by the State: A pension of 1/140 of the final compensation [average compensation of the last five years of service] multiplied by the total number of years of service rendered prior to the date of retirement.
2. Provided by Employee: An annuity of approximately 1/140 of the final compensation multiplied by the number of years of service rendered while the employee was contributing to the retirement plan.
3. Additional Allowance by the State to Present Employees: An

---

1 *State of New York, Report of the Commission on Pensions, March 30, 1920* (Albany, New York: J. B. Lyon Co., 1920) , pp. 21–22.

additional pension of 1/140 of the final compensation multiplied by the number of years of service rendered prior to the establishment of the retirement system. This benefit will provide the annuity which the employee would otherwise have provided by past contributions on account of this service.[2]

This formula[3] resulted in a mixture of what would currently be called a *defined benefit* plan and a form of a *defined contribution* plan (the latter is sometimes called a *money purchase* plan). The annuity[4] portion of the retirement allowance is derived from the *defined contribution* of the employee, the accumulation of which is converted to its actuarial equivalent in monthly annuity. This annuity is supplemented by a pension, provided by employer money, in an amount directly related to the salary and service of the retiring employee. Thus the pension portion of the formula is categorized as a "defined benefit" plan.

For a substantial majority of employees covered by public employee retirement systems in the U.S. and Canada, retirement benefits are computed on the basis of defined benefit formulas. In many instances, this type of formula has evolved over the years from a defined contribution approach. An example of the evolution is found in the California Public Employees' Retirement System, one of the largest public employee systems, with over 400,000 members.

When originally established in 1931, the California system provided for employee contributions similar to those of the original New York system and the present New Jersey system (see Table 1). The employer portion of the benefit matched in pension what the accumulated contributions of the em-

---

2 Ibid., p. 24.

3 The 1920 New York formula has been phased out in recent years, as a result of changes which caused the New York State Employees' Retirement System to become noncontributory for most of its members.

4 Some of the terms used in the New York report have acquired specialized meanings which are now in common use in public employee retirement jargon. Following are some abbreviated definitions:

1. *Pension:* bought by the employer.
2. *Annuity:* bought by the employee.
3. *Retirement allowance:* the sum of pension and annuity.

ployee provided when converted to an annuity. In 1947 the law was amended, leaving the pattern of employee contributions basically unchanged but converting the total retirement allowance to a defined benefit basis. If the goals of the new program were precisely met, the contributions of an employee whose entire service was under the formula would accumulate at retirement to the amount necessary to provide one half of the retirement allowance, the employer being responsible for the balance. However, even if these goals were not met, the total benefit payment was still as scheduled, and the employer had to provide whatever pension was necessary to supplement the benefit provided by the accumulated employee contributions. This might require a contribution of the employer which more than matches the employee's contributions, or it could require less than matching. In any event, the employee could plan his retirement finances around the level of benefit which he had been led to believe would be his. The final stage in the evolution took place in 1971 in connection with an improvement in the benefit level. At that time, the employee contribution rate was changed to a uniform 7 percent of salary from a schedule graded by sex and by age at entry.[5]

The liberalization of benefits referred to in the previous paragraph brought the basic benefit under the California system up to one half of final salary upon retirement at age 60 with 25 years of service. The basic benefit is reduced by $2.67 per month (or somewhat less for low-paid employees) for each year the retired employee was covered by social security. Anyone with at least 5 years of service can retire at age 60, but if his service is other than 25 years, his benefit will be proportionately increased or reduced. For comparison, the New York system provides a retirement benefit of half salary for an employee of the state who retires at age 55 with 25 years of service, with corresponding reductions for persons with lower periods of service. These two systems cover several

---

[5] For employees with social security coverage, the present 7 percent rate applies to salary in excess of $400 per month, the rate being 4.67 percent on the first $400 of monthly salary.

hundred thousand employees each and between them provide benefits to about 10 percent of the total nonfederal public employees covered by retirement systems in the United States and Canada. It is important to note that the benefits provided by these two systems are more generous than those of many other public employee retirement systems.

Defined Contribution versus Defined Benefit. The distinction between a defined contribution and defined benefit plan is not always readily apparent but can be of vital importance. The difference between the original California and New York systems illustrates this. Both systems embraced the concept that a portion of the total benefit at retirement would be provided by converting the employee's accumulated contributions into an annuity. The employee contribution rates were set to develop the desired annuity so long as salary growth and interest earnings were experienced as assumed. Both systems also were designed to have the employer purchase a pension of an amount equal to the annuity. In the original California plan, the matching was to be precise.

If the annuity were greater or less than the original objective, the pension would be correspondingly changed. In the original New York plan, on the other hand, the pension was specifically defined to be the desired amount. The difference in results between the two methods occurred when interest earnings or an employee's salary history differed over the years from the levels anticipated in setting his contribution rates. Under such circumstances, the employee's annuity would not equal the amount the program was designed to provide. Despite this, the objective of the original New York formula would still be met by the pension, since it was calculated as a defined benefit; only the annuity, on a defined contribution basis, would stray from the mark. Under the original California system, where the employer-paid pension at retirement was set equal to the annuity provided by the employee's contributions, when the annuity was off (as it nearly always was), so also was the pension.

This example illustrates one clear-cut advantage of a

defined benefit formula: It focuses upon the major purpose of a retirement system—providing benefits. A defined benefit formula fosters employee acceptance and appreciation for a program of retirement benefits, because the projected benefits are easily estimated. In addition, the benefit formula can be more precisely tailored to fit the objectives of the program. For example, many systems use a progressive benefit formula, one which provides a specified percentage of salary as a retirement benefit for each of the first 10 or 15 years, and a higher percentage for each of the subsequent years of service. This type of formula gives a premium for long service with the employer and is only feasible when a defined benefit formula is used. Similarly, only by the use of a defined benefit formula can minimum benefits be provided, to assure that persons meeting certain age and service specifications receive a specified level of benefit regardless of what they would otherwise receive according to the regular benefit formula.

A defined contribution formula also has certain intrinsic advantages. In the first place, insofar as it is applicable to annuities derived from accumulated employee contributions, it is obviously equitable to the employee. Where the employer-purchased pension is also on a defined contribution basis, the employer has a firm fix on his commitments to finance the retirement program. This approach also instills and reinforces a sense of employer-employee partnershp in providing the retirement benefits. A defined contribution formula of this sort further facilitates an equitable and understandable provision to vest all or a portion of an employer's contributions upon an employee's termination prior to retirement.

A major disadvantage of a defined contribution formula is that a uniform rate of contributions for all employees is inherently incapable of meeting most benefit goals, such as those of the original New York report with respect to the annuity to be purchased from accumulated contributions. Instead, the contribution rate must vary by age, sex, and sometimes occupational class. A schedule of contributions of this type is used by the New Jersey Public Employees' Retirement System (Table 1). The need for this type of schedule is not always clear to the employees making the larger contributions but is based on elementary actuarial principles.

Over the years, interest on an employee's contributions is accumulated and added to the contributions themselves. At his retirement, the total is converted to an annuity. The interest portion of the accumulated total contributions for an employee with a long period of participation in the system is relatively large; the interest portion for an employee with a short period of participation is relatively small. This is because the contributions made in each of the earlier years of an employee's career earn more interest than those made near the end. If the annuity is to be directly proportionate to the period of service, as the New York formula calls for, a larger percentage contribution is required for an employee entering service later in life, to make up for the loss of long-term interest on his contributions. Hence, the variation in contribution rates by age.

In converting the accumulated employee contributions at retirement to an annuity, the differences in mortality between men and women (and, occasionally and to a much lesser extent, between occupational classes of employees) may be recognized. Since women have a longer life expectancy than men, a larger fund at retirement is required to support the same annuity benefit. Thus, the variation in contribution rates by sex.

The rates of employee contribution may be geared to produce annuities proportionate to the final salaries of the employees, rather than to their salaries over their entire working career. If this is done, future salary increases should be anticipated. The salaries of clerical employees tend to increase by age and tenure, for example, while wages for hourly employees are largely independent of age. For this reason, the contributions needed from clerical employees in the early years of their careers might represent a higher percentage of earnings than those needed from hourly employees, in order to provide sufficient funds at retirement to reflect the larger expected salaries of the clerical employees at that time. Consequently, some systems require higher contributions from clerical and administrative employees than from certain other classes of employees, such as laborers.

Career Average versus Final Salary. Many systems, especially smaller ones, use a defined contribution formula for determining a portion of the total retirement allowance. This is accomplished by converting accumulated employee contributions to annuities at retirement. This approach was once quite common but is becoming less popular. For determining the remainder of the retirement allowance, the employer-paid pension, the defined contribution method is even rarer. Its declining popularity in both instances is closely related to its tendency to produce retirement benefits which are disproportionately weighted by the salary history of an employee early in his working career. Because of this, the defined contribution method has characteristics similar to those of a defined benefit formula using a *career average salary* method.

In a typical formula employing career average salaries, a unit of benefit based on the salary earned during that year is credited for each year of service, the total benefit being the sum of such units. While a few public employee retirement systems use such a method, the vast majority use a *final average salary* method. Under the final salary method, the benefit is computed by multiplying the final salary by the product of the benefit percentage and the years of credited service. The final average salary is usually defined as the compensation earned by the retiring member during a relatively short period of years (commonly three or five) either at the end of his working career or at the high point of his earnings. In periods of rapidly rising wages, the shorter the period used for the average, the less the average is brought down by the inclusion of earlier, low salary years. For this reason, in plans using a final salary formula, there is continuing pressure from employee groups for a reduction in the length of the period used in the final salary base, as an indirect means of raising benefits.

Some systems have gone to the extreme of defining final salary as precisely the salary of the employee on his date of termination. This technique is particularly applicable to police and fire systems, where the rank and salary status of an employee is generally clearly defined. Final rank salary certainly reflects final compensation patterns accurately. However, it also risks the artificial inflation of pension benefits by means of substantial promotions given immediately prior to retirement or by the heaping of vacation, overtime, and other supplemental pay into the final salary. Specific legislation has been enacted in New York state to prevent this type of abuse.

Annuity Conversion Rates. In many public employee retirement systems, a participant's contributions, accumulated with interest to his retirement, are converted to monthly annuities which are added to the pension to comprise the total retirement allowance. Where this is the case, the schedule of rates at which the contributions are converted into annuities is a matter of great consequence to the retiring employee. In order to put into focus the issues involved in establishing such a schedule, the criteria to be met by a schedule of conversion rates must be reviewed.

The conversion of accumulated contributons to an annuity is comparable to purchasing an annuity from an insurance company. The conversion or purchase rate for a retiring employee is based on an assumed interest rate and an assumed longevity. This assumed interest rate is usually based on an estimate of the interest rate likely to be earned by the system in the future. The assumed longevity typically varies by age at retirement and by sex. Younger retirees are assumed to live longer than older retirees, and women are assumed to live longer than men. Hence, a conversion rate schedule usually will provide a higher annuity for each $1000 of accumulated contributions to a retiring man who is age 65 than to one who is age 60, and a higher annuity to a retiring man than to a woman the same age.

An equitable schedule of conversion rates might thus be defined as one which leaves the total funds of the systems in balance before and after converting contributions into annuities, regardless of the longevity of the retirees or the interest earned on the system's funds. Consider a group of annuitants who retire the same day and whose accumulated contributions are placed in a hypothetical savings account, which is augmented only by interest and depleted only by payment of the group's annuities. Ideally, the aggregate level of annuity payments to the group would be set so that the savings account would be fully depleted by the last payment made to the last surviving annuitant in the group. It is not statistically possible to predict interest and mortality rates with sufficient accuracy to meet such an ideal. Nevertheless, the goal can be met approximately, particularly if adjustments are made in the rates from time to time to correct for previous inaccuracies. The system's funds can be treated much the same as if the system were a mutual life insurance company whose goal is to pay out, in the long run, all of the accumulated employee contributions in the form of annuities.

Unfortunately, certain practical considerations can frustrate the attainment of the ideal. Many systems are too small to achieve the proper spread of risk. The ideal requires statistical records to be maintained in sufficient detail to allow accurate measurement of the appropriateness of the conversion rates. This can be beyond the technical capabilities of some systems. In addition, a change in conversion rates may be resisted simply because of the corresponding change in the total benefit payable. Nevertheless, if conversion rates are to remain equitable, rate changes reducing future annuities will occur of annuitants' life expectancies increase. Additional interest earnings may offset improved longevity on occasion but cannot consistently do so.

Modifications in annuity conversion rates generally affect all subsequent retirements, in order to reflect current experience promptly. In some systems, however, legal restrictions may prevent this practice. In these systems annuity rates cannot be changed with respect to any employee after he enters the system. Under these circumstances, the amount of an employee's annuity may be determined by the mortality experience of retirees 25 to 40 years or more prior to his retirement. To compound the obvious difficulties of establishing proper rates so far in advance, this type of restriction on changing rates tend to arise as a result of litigation, rather than from explicit statutory direction. The system may be taken by surprise and be unable to allow for future improvements in mortality for an entire generation of members. The resulting losses to the system must either be charged to subsequent generations of annuitants or be made up by the employer.

A less serious, but still significant, problem exists where the conversion rates of annuities are fixed for all contributions made while the rates were in effect. In this situation a system may change its rates with respect to future contributions, but must freeze the rates with respect to all contributions received before the date of change of rate.

BENEFIT ENTITLEMENT

In order to receive retirement benefits, an employee must meet certain requirements as to age, period of credited service with the system, or both. In a private plan, an employee meeting these requirements is called eligible for "normal retirement," or is said to have reached his "normal retirement date." These phrases are not so widely used in this sense among public employee retirement systems.

In public systems the most common phrase used for retirement without special eligibility (such as disability) is "service retirement." This term is inadequate in the usual case where there is a minimum age requirement for retirement. A similar failing exists for the somewhat more descriptive but less common term "age retirement," since most systems have minimum service requirements for retirement. "Superannuation" is the most descriptive word of all but has become obsolescent, perhaps because it seems ponderous. In order to conform to language used in private plans, and to settle upon a single term, the phrase *normal retirement* will be used to refer to an employee's terminating employment and receiving the regular formula benefits of a retirement system without special qualifications, such as disability. Similarly, *normal retirement date* will be used in defining the earliest possible date an employee can qualify for normal retirement. In this sense, normal retirement will be distinguished from disability retirement or early retirement. The phrases *age retirement* and *service retirement* will be reserved for specific reference to eligibility for benefits dependent only upon age or service, respectively.[6]

Because of the interplay of age and service requirements for normal retirement, in some systems there is no specific age at which retirement is to be expected. This is particularly true in a system where normal retirement is available at a relatively young age and where the employee is also accruing benefits under a federal old-age benefit program. Many employees in this situation will continue to work until eligible for both the local and federal benefit on an unreduced basis. Even where a federal benefit is not available, there will not necessarily be a rush to retire at the earliest possible age, since there will normally be a substantial difference between a retiring employee's salary and his retirement allowance. Thus, an employee's normal retirement date is not the date he is expected to retire, but rather the date he is first eligible for an unreduced benefit.

Age Requirements.   The magic number for retirement has long been 65, particularly since the social security systems of the United States and Canada provide their basic benefits at that age. Private pension plans, most of which have had their greatest growth while under the influence of the federal systems, have largely used age 65 as the normal retirement date. In recent years, however, there has been a definite trend toward earlier retirement ages.[7]

---

6 The phrase "normal retirement" is also occasionally used in connection with optional retirement forms to indicate the automatic or standard form, which is generally a lifetime allowance. For additional remarks in the area of terminology, see Municipal Finance Officers Association, *Public Employee Retirement Terminology* (Chicago, 1956).

7 Further evidence of the ambiguity of the phrase "normal retirement" is given by a 1970 study by the Bankers Trust Company, New York. Although

In the area of public employment, the availability of unreduced benefits upon retirement at an age earlier than 65 has been prevalent in the United States for some time. In Canada, age 65 still predominates as the youngest age for normal retirement for general employees in public employee retirement systems. In both countries, policemen and firefighters have traditionally become eligible for normal retirement at a significantly younger age than other public employees, primarily because of the strenuous nature of their duties. While a majority of United States systems allow normal retirement for general employees at ages near 60, the earliest age for normal retirement for policemen and firefighters is usually between 50 and 55.[8]

Service Requirements.   The concept of benefit entitlement on the sole basis of service, regardless of age, has been accepted for some time in certain sectors of public employment. For example, in both the United States and Canada the military retirement programs define normal retirement in terms of period of service. In similar fashion, a large number of policemen and firefighters have years of service as the primary determinant for their normal retirement date. Among general public employees, although age retirement still predominates, service retirement with an unreduced benefit is often available after 30 or 35 years of credited service.

This type of service retirement, where an unreduced service retirement allowance is available regardless of age, should be distinguished from a requirement that a certain minimum amount of service be completed at normal retirement. An example of the latter is a provision that an employee must

more than 90 percent of the plans of the 201 companies surveyed had a "normal retirement age" of 65, the early retirement provisions of a significant number of these plans provided full accrued benefits to early retirees without reduction. See Bankers Trust Company, *Study of Industrial Retirement Plans* (New York, 1970), pp. 13–17 and 25–26.

[8] Social Security Administration Research Report No. 15: *State and Local Government Retirement Systems, 1965* and Research Report No. 23: *Retirement Systems for Employees of State and Local Governments, 1966*, and the author's sampling of Canadian systems.

have completed 10 years of service and attained age 60 for normal retirement. For the bulk of the employees, those hired prior to age 50, the governing condition is still the attainment of age 60. Such a combination of both age and service requirement for normal retirement is common, particularly among systems covering general employees, as contrasted with policemen and firefighters.

As noted earlier, in many systems for policemen and firefighters, the normal retirement date is defined in terms of service alone. This is substantially equivalent to a definition using age alone, because participants in these systems tend to enter public employment within a narrow age range in their mid-20s. For example, if most members of such a system should enter within a year of their 24th birthdays, a 30-year service requirement for normal retirement is equivalent to a normal retirement age of 54 or so.

Compulsory Retirement.   Most public employees covered by retirement systems are subject to compulsory retirement at some age. Such a provision has the advantage of removing the burden from the employer of determining when employees must retire, thereby improving his relationship with older employees and opening up positions for the younger employees. A compulsory retirement provision may categorically allow no employment beyond a certain age or it may require specific employer approval of continued employment beyond that age. In systems covering elected officials, exceptions to compulsory retirement generally allow the election of any person to office, regardless of age.

FORM OF PAYMENT

The simplest form of retirement allowance is paid monthly to the retiring employee, starting at his retirement and ceasing upon his death. Aside from the possibility of reduction or suspension of benefits during any period of reemployment, the retirement allowance is generally fully vested in the employee upon his retirement.

Retirement systems normally provide several alternate

forms for the receipt of the regular retirement allowance. The monthly amount of the optional benefit is usually at such level that it is the *actuarial equivalent* of the regular benefit it replaces. This means that the optional benefit is generally lower in amount than the regular benefit, the difference being the value, as determined actuarially, of the additional benefit payable because of the option. The election of an alternate form is the prerogative of the employee. However, some systems impose administrative restrictions on the timing of the election, to prevent an employee from choosing an option which could adversely affect the financial condition of the system. For example, an employee might be required to elect his option two years before retirement, so as to keep any employee whose health becomes poor thereafter from choosing an option strictly for the purpose of increasing the total amount of benefit paid to him or his beneficiary. Despite this hazard and the additional benefit cost, many systems have eliminated this type of restriction and allow the election of an option any time prior to retirement. This more generous practice is easier to administer and improves employee acceptance of the retirement program.

Payment for Period Certain and Life. One common form of payment, which may be either the basic benefit of the system or an optional alternative, is a retirement allowance which continues for a certain period of years, whether or not the employee survives that period. If the employee dies within that period, payments continue to the employee's beneficiary for the remainder of the period. If the employee survives beyond that period, the benefit continues thereafter so long as he remains alive. The period may be a specified number of years, such as ten years. Alternatively, it may be of such length as to guarantee that the employee's accumulated contributions at retirement will be returned in total benefit payments or, in some systems, in employee-purchased annuity payments. These alternative forms are called a *modified refund annuity* and *refund annuity* respectively. Frequently, the balance guaranteed is paid after the employee's death as a lump sum instead of as monthly payments.

Continuation to Surviving Beneficiary.   Another form of optional benefit widely available in public employee retirement systems allows a retired employee's benefit to be continued to his named beneficiary after his death. The amount of the continued payment is either the same as before the employee's death or a specified fraction of that amount. Payments continue only if the beneficiary survives the employee and then for the beneficiary's lifetime. The most common use of this option is by a husband and wife, to assure that payments continue to the death of the last survivor. This option often provides a pattern for the payment of monthly benefits upon the death of an employee prior to normal retirement.

Standard Form.   The form of benefit provided automatically can be an important consideration in comparing the benefit level of two systems. One form of benefit is a life-only allowance, which terminates upon the death of the retired person. A more valuable form of benefit provides that payments will continue after the retiree's death until his accumulated contributons have been returned, either in monthly payments or in cash. The dollar value of the death benefit is generally small—1 or 2 percent of the total value of the retirement allowance, on the average—but its worth to the individual's estate in the event of an early death can be quite substantial. Moreover, this method avoids the personnel and public relations problems which can arise where most of an employee's contributions are forfeited due to early death.

In some systems, particularly in those providing benefits for policemen and firefighters, the automatic form of payment is a lifetime allowance which continues at the same or a related level to the employee's spouse after his death. Although this benefit is generally available as an option in most systems, the price the employee pays for it in terms of reduced monthly allowance can be quite substantial, ranging up to a 30 percent reduction or so. Where the benefit is provided automatically, the value of the basic retirement allowance is correspondingly enhanced.

Suspension during Reemployment. In nearly all systems, benefits are reduced or suspended if the retiree returns to employment within the system or, in some cases, to public employment within the state or province. There appear to be no systems under which a retired employee will adversely affect his retirement benefits by public employment outside the system's state or province, or by private employment anywhere. The restrictions on reemployment within the system, or in other local public employment, vary in severity among the systems. In some systems, such reemployment after retirement is absolutely prohibited. A more generous provision allows reemployment, during which time the benefit is suspended but no additional credit is accrued. Even more generous provisions allow additional benefits to accrue or pensions to continue during reemployment.

Reemployment on a part-time or temporary basis after retirement poses similar problems of equitable treatment. The most common example of this type of reemployment involves retired teachers who are available as substitutes for some period of time after retirement. Reemployment provisions in retirement systems are often designed to accommodate this arrangement, since it is generally to the advantage of both retired teachers and school systems to have retired teachers substitute on a limited scale. A common provision allows a retired teacher to maintain his pension while substituting up to a certain specified number of days during a year, the number often falling in the 45–90 day range, with 60 days being a frequent allowance. In some systems, the restrictions are liberalized as the age or the length of time the teacher has been retired increases, in a manner similar to the work restrictions of United States social security.

Another common provision governing reemployment sets a maximum on the salary which can be earned in employment covered by the system without forfeiting retirement benefits, again paralleling the rules under social security. Utah teachers, for example, are subject to the same earnings limitations for reemployment in positions covered by their retirement system as are used for social security.

POSTRETIREMENT ADJUSTMENTS

The traditional concept of the retirement benefit is one in fixed dollars: Once the employee has retired and the amount of his retirement allowance has been determined, no change in the schedule of monthly payments is contemplated. This concept has probably never been entirely satisfactory. The erosion by inflation of the purchasing power of a fixed dollar pension is well recognized, but it has only been in recent years that positive steps to correct this deficiency have been taken. Public employee retirement systems have been in the forefront of this movement.

As the rest of this chapter will show, many different approaches are being used to ease the effects of inflation on the budgets of retired persons. Most of these methods are designed to keep retirement benefits in step with changes in the cost of living. A more far-reaching program that is occasionally discussed makes adjustments for changes in living standards. Actually neither the term *cost of living* nor the term *living standard* is subject to adequate objective definition, since life styles are continuously changing. For example, at the beginning of this century, public transportation played a large role in determining how people lived, so that ease of access to public transportation was a major determinant of a family's living standard. At the present, access to public transportation has become a minor element in living standards. Its place has been taken by the automobile which has revolutionized transportation and become a major factor in present day living standards. An index using either public transportation or the automobile over this span of time as measures of living cost would have failed to reflect the changing patterns of life style.

One might illustrate the concepts involved as they apply to postretirement adjustments as follows: A 1955 pensioner wishing to replace his black-and-white television set in 1970 might buy a radio if he has had no postretirement adjustments, or buy another black-and-white television if he has had a cost of living adjustment, or buy a color TV if he has had a living standards adjustment.

Need for Adjustments. The most widely recognized measure of cost of living in the United States and Canada is the consumer price index. Using each country's index as a guide, retirement allowances would have had to be adjusted by the percentages shown in Table 2 in order to provide a benefit in 1970 with the same purchasing power as the pension when it began. Thus a U.S. pensioner drawing $100 a month at his retirement in 1940 would need $277 per month in 1970 to obtain the same value in goods and services, as measured by the consumer price index.

The blends of goods and services whose changes in price are measured in the indexes used in Table 2 are not the same

TABLE 2
1970 Consumer Price Index as Percentage of Index in Selected Years

Year	United States	Canada
1970 .... 100%		100%
1960 131		131
1950 161		163
1940 277		255
1930 232		223

as those normally required by retired persons. In Canada, the Pension Index was started in 1967 to measure the change in pensioner's living costs. It is used to provide an automatic adjustment in the benefits under the Canada Pension Plan. No comparable index exists in the United States. However, a background study of various possible methods of making automatic adjustments to social security benefits led to the conclusion that a specialized index for retired persons is not currently necessary.[9] Among other reasons cited for this conclusion was a report showing that "even in a period when larger-than-average price changes tended to be concentrated

---

[9] Daniel N. Price and Robert O. Brunner, "Automatic Adjustment of OASDHI Cash Benefits," *Social Security Bulletin* (May 1970) , pp. 3–11.

in classes of items which are relatively more important in the spending pattern of older consumers, the total change was not substantially larger for older than young families."[10]

An index to show the increase in living standards might follow wage rates or productivity, rather than prices. In his book on postretirement adjustments, John P. Mackin presents a table[11] based on several of these types of indexes. This table shows the changes in these indexes of living standards for the decade ending in 1969. These indexes exhibited growth rates in this decade ranging from 39 percent to 68 percent, depending upon the type of index. Since the consumer price index rose 26 percent during the same period, these indexes of living standards increased from 50 percent to 160 percent faster than did the consumer price index during the same period.

Regardless of the index adopted, if any, to measure the change in value of the monthly allowance, the method used to determine the original amount of the allowance is of great significance. A career average-salary formula is probably out of date at retirement, in terms of matching the retiring employee's income needs after retirement to the salaries and the price level at that date. This is particularly likely if a short period of sharply rising wages has occurred within a few years prior to retirement, since the bulk of the average retirement benefit will be based on earnings at earlier lower levels. On the other hand, benefits based on final average salaries will tend to be up-to-date with respect to wage rate changes occurring during the retiree's period of employment. For this reason any postretirement adjustment procedure which attempts to follow an index will meet its objective better when used with a final average salary plan than with a career average plan.

---

10 Helen H. Lamale, "The Impact of Rising Prices on Younger and Older Consumers," BLS Report No. 238–2, December 1963.

11 John P. Mackin, *Protecting Purchasing Power in Retirement* (New York: Fleet Academic Editions, Inc., 1971), Table III–8. This book provides a thorough analysis of postretirement programs in public employee retirement systems.

A postretirement adjustment procedure may give rise to an anomaly if the basic benefit to be adjusted is flat; that is, not dependent upon salary. A minimum benefit is often of that nature; for example, $100 per month for anyone retiring with at least 20 years of service, regardless of salary. The anomaly results if such a benefit for someone already retired is increased, even though a current retiree gets only the unadjusted benefit. This inequity may be avoided either by not making flat benefits subject to postretirement adjustments, or by increasing the benefits for retired lives and making corresponding improvements in the flat benefits provided for those currently retiring.

Scope of Adjustment. The programs of postretirement adjustments in use have a number of variations in their scope. In order to discuss these variations, it will be helpful to define the following terms:

Ad hoc refers to a single increase in the amount of current monthly payments to each affected retired person.

Automatic refers to adjustments in benefits on a recurring regular basis.

An additional concept needed to define the scope of a program of postretirement adjustments is its applicability. The program may cover only retired persons, perhaps even excluding certain types of these, such as those retired for disability. Alternatively, a program may include all employees, both active and retired. Similarly, adjustments may be applicable to the entire retirement allowance, or only to the employer-bought pension or the employee-bought annuity. In another area, the adjustment may be inapplicable to flat benefits or minimum benefits.

Although other combinations are possible, most arrangements for postretirement adjustment of benefits fall into one of the following categories:

1. Ad hoc adjustment of allowances for retired lives without automatic adjustments thereafter.
2. Ad hoc adjustment of allowances for retired lives with automatic adjustments thereafter for them.

3. Ad hoc adjustment of allowances for retired lives with automatic adjustments thereafter both for them and for future retirees.

The first of these categories is probably the most commonly used. Under it, the allowances of some or all of the retired persons under a system, will be adjusted as of the effective date of the governing legislation. After that date, the amounts of all allowances will remain as adjusted without further change. The retirement allowance of any person retiring subsequent to that date would not be affected by the ad hoc adjustment.

The second category is like the first, except that the retirement allowances are subject to automatic adjustments on a regular basis after the ad hoc adjustment is effected. For example, a program of this type might call for an immediate increase of all allowances for presently retired employees of $2 per month for each year since retirement. In addition, an automatic increase of $2 per month would be made each year in the future for those same retirees. If the monthly allowance of a person who has been retired ten years is $100, it would be immediately increased to $120 under such a program. One year later it would go up to $122, and be subject to additional increases of $2 each year thereafter.

The third category has the features of the method just described and also provides for similar adjustments to be made in the retirement allowances of presently active employees upon their retirement. This technique is comprehensive in scope since it provides automatically for the postretirement adjustments to be made in the future.

Programs involving an ad hoc adjustment for retired persons are generally on a nonretroactive basis. Benefits are adjusted after the procedure takes effect, but no lump sum adjustments are made for earlier monthly benefits. This avoids giving a windfall to the retirees and also avoids many administrative problems, particularly with respect to pensioners whose benefits terminated prior to the adjustment.

The ad hoc method of updating has been used frequently

under the U.S. social security program, with obvious political implications. When Congress makes an adjustment in retired life benefits, it creates an aura of goodwill which is not intended to discourage the voter from expressing his gratitude. In the Canada Pension Plan, on the other hand, a continuing form of adjustment for active and retired employees has been in effect since the Plan's inception. In 1972, a similar automatic program was adopted in the United States. Although this method does not generate the same periodic political dividends, it has the advantage of producing orderly and predictable adjustments.

Among public employees' retirement systems, the motivation for the ad hoc method has not been merely political. The financing of any postretirement adjustment program can be a significant consideration in determining whether it should be adopted. With an ad hoc adjustment, the costs can be defined with some precision. Where the proposal involves automatic increases in the future, especially increases related to an index such as the consumer price index, the cost of the adoption of the program of postretirement adjustments can be not only large but also difficult to predict. For this reason, some legislative bodies prefer to make adjustments only after the amount of the adjustment can be spelled out precisely, rather than to adopt a program of automatic adjustments.

In systems where the employee's accumulated contributions are converted into annuities, the adjustment may be limited to the employer-purchased pension. Limiting any increase to the pension portion of the retirement allowance obviously costs less than increasing both the pension and the employee-bought annuity. Where the cost of the adjustment is met by the employer, restricting the adjustment to the pensions may also reflect a philosophy limiting the employer's commitment to the cost of pensions. This philosophy would not contemplate adjustment of annuities without additional employee contribution.

Mechanisms of Adjustment. The term *scope* is used to embrace the concepts just discussed: the applicability of a program of postretirement adjustments, as to both the persons affected and the portions of their allowances modified, and whether benefits are to be adjusted on an ad hoc basis or whether automatic adjustments in the future are contemplated. Another method of classification is what will be termed the *mechanism* of a postretirement adjustment program. The mechanism embodies the method by which the specific amount of adjustment can be determined for each affected person.

Among the mechanisms available, the following are the ones most commonly found in public employee retirement systems:

1. *Nonproportional.* A flat dollar amount is added to each monthly benefit, or deficient benefit amounts are raised to meet a specified minimum based upon the period of active service, or some other similar improvement in benefit is provided.

2. *Percentage increase.* The benefit is increased a certain percent, commonly 1.5 or 2 percent each year. This may be compounded, but is generally not, resulting in the same dollar amount of increase for any particular employee each year.

3. *Index-related.* The benefit is adjusted periodically in the same proportion as the change in an index, such as the consumer price index.

4. *Salary-related.* The benefit is adjusted periodically in the same proportion as the change in the salary of the position held by the pensioner when he retired, either according to his actual rank or position at retirement, or according to a salary average in his general employment classification.

5. *Yield-adjusted.* The benefit is adjusted periodically according to the investment experience of an allocated portion of the assets, generally common stocks, held to support the benefit.

Many programs combine two or more of these mechanisms. For example, an adjustment program used in many large systems provides that the retirement allowance will be increased by 1.5 or 2 percent each year, provided that the consumer price index has increased by at least that amount during that year. Another method, used by the Idaho and North Carolina public employee retirement systems, adjusts retirement allowances on a continuing basis, based on the consumer price index but subject to a limit of a 3 percent annual increase and only if the assets have grown sufficiently to warrant the increase, as decided by the governing boards. The mechanism is thus a combination of a percentage increase, an index-related and a yield-adjusted method.

The nonproportional category of adjustments includes programs which give to retired persons the benefits of changes in the formulas determining retirement allowances for active members. In such a program, a basic increase in the level of benefit or an increased minimum benefit might be passed along to retired as well as active persons. Although such a practice has obvious merit, its cost can also impede future adjustments in benefits if it establishes a precedent which must be followed.

A program of continuing postretirement adjustments which employs a percentage increase mechanism can match the changes in cost of living only approximately. In a period of rapidly increasing cost of living, a comparison of the adjustments generated by such a program with the increases in the consumer price index might bring pressures for additional postretirement increases. These additional increases may be granted on an ad hoc basis, without affecting the rate of future scheduled increases. Alternatively, the percentage to be used for future annual increases may be changed. This latter method may lead the system into a one-way street, where it is not possible to revert to the original rate of increases when the cost of living levels out. Obviously this type of program could be very expensive in the long run.

An index-related mechanism enjoys the advantage of easy acceptance by the employees, the employers, and the public, particularly where the index is in common use, such as the consumer price index. Since a postretirement adjustment program has as its basic objective the protection of the purchasing power of the retired employee, its success in meeting this objective will often be measured by the use of an index such as the consumer price index. Accordingly there is a practical advantage in tying the adjustment mechanism to the index that will be used to judge it.

Similarly, salary-related mechanisms are easily understood and widely accepted, particularly among public employees. They tend to be quite costly, however, and this has limited the extent of their adoption. The most prevalent systems using the salary-related mechanism are those covering policemen and firefighters. The benefit is often defined as a specified percentage of the salary attaching to the rank from which the pensioner retired, the retirement benefit varying in amount in the same proportion as does the salary. Thus, the benefits for a group of pensioners will tend to change as the general salary scale in the police or fire department changes. This fact leads to a major disadvantage of this mechanism: Since increases in salaries result in increases in pensions, the budgetary hurdle associated with pay boosts is higher than usual. The postretirement increase program might thus serve to hobble salary adjustments for the active employee.

A yield-adjusted retirement benefit commonly takes the form of a *variable* or *equity annuity*. Under a program using this mechanism, the benefit rises or falls as the value of a portfolio of securities, generally common stocks, rises or falls. Equity annuities are often provided at the employee's option, as an alternative to a conventional, fixed-benefit annuity. Because of the volatility of common stock portfolios, it is usual for only a portion of the total retirement allowance to be varied, often that portion of the benefit produced by the accumulated employee contributions. The balance of the benefit is generally in a fixed amount. Thus, the combined retirement allowance is not subject to the degree of fluctuation which the equity annuity by itself experiences, and a limit is placed on the risk of the entire benefit's being drastically reduced under poor market conditions. In effect, the employee is "gambling" only his own money, the employer-purchased pension being unaffected by gains and losses of the equity annuity fund.

Under a typical equity annuity program, each participating employee's contributions are accumulated in the equity portfolio, rather than at the system's fixed rate of interest. His accumulated contributions at retirement are then converted into an equity annuity. If the equity accumulation is larger than the accumulation would have been at the fixed interest rate, the annuitant starts out with a higher annuity. Thereafter, his annuity rises or falls depending on whether the equity portfolio's rate of return is higher or lower than the fixed interest rate. Based on past performances of broad portfolios of common stock, the retired employee with such an equity annuity may expect to receive more over his remaining lifetime from the equity annuity than he would have received from the fixed-dollar annuity it replaces.

Over many extended periods of time, common stock prices have increased more than the cost of living. Since equity annuities follow the trends of common stock values objections to equity annuities are generally few during periods of rising stock values, but more numerous and more vocal when the stock market has been declining. Particularly difficult are those periods when the stock market is declining, while the cost of living is increasing. A related disadvantage of equity annuities is that the employee bears the entire investment risk, at least with respect to the portion of his benefit subject to adjustment. In contrast, the system retains the investment risk under other forms of postretirement adjustment. Additional objections to equity annuities are that they are complicated, and that it is difficult to explain to the average retiring employee the nature of his benefit and the risks he is taking. For this reason, the equity annuity has found its largest acceptance in the more sophisticated groups of public employees, especially teachers.

Another form of yield-adjusted benefit pays to pensioners all or a portion of the excess interest earnings on the system's funds. The payment may be made in the form of increased monthly payments or it may involve a *thirteenth check,* an additional payment at the end of the fiscal year. The excess interest earnings may arise because of capital gains on investments in common stocks or because of interest in excess of that nominally required to maintain the financial soundness of the system. To the extent that the latter is the case, this method places an undue emphasis upon the somewhat arbitrary decision as to assumed future interest earnings.[12] It might, in fact, impede modernization of the assumptions if such modernization were to result in an increase in the assumed interest rate. Such an increase would decrease future payments of the asset-adjusted type by allocating a larger portion of the actual interest earnings to meeting the assumed interest rate. Moreover, while the provision of increased benefits from capital gains on equities might tend to result in increases related to the cost of living, it would generally be coincidental for excess interest to increase in proportion to the increase in the cost of living.

---

12 See p. 93.

Chapter 4

The Total Benefit Structure

RETIREMENT SYSTEMS come in many sizes and shapes, from small programs designed solely to provide normal retirement benefits to complex systems providing protection against nearly any adverse contingency that could befall an employee during his working career. In the latter portion of this chapter, various criteria will be given for evaluating such benefit structures, including broad comparisons of benefits provided by public employee retirement systems and plans in the private sector. Earlier, the chapter will consider elements of the benefit structure other than normal retirement, to complement the discussion of the previous chapter.

EMPLOYEE RIGHTS PRIOR TO NORMAL RETIREMENT

Over the years that public employee retirement systems have been in existence, normal retirement benefits have been augmented by other related benefits. Most public employee programs presently include provisions for cash payments or monthly income benefits in the event of disablement (occupational or nonoccupational), death (either before or after retirement), or other severance of employment.

Disability Benefits. Protection against disability is almost universally available to public employees covered by retirement systems, once certain age and service requirements have been met. In fact, about four out of five employees have become eligible for this coverage when they have ten years of service, and about one third in the police and fire category in the United States are immediately eligible.[1]

Not only do policemen and firefighters become protected by disability benefits very early in their careers, but often they are provided pensions with disablements that are not as severe as required for pensions to be paid to other classes of employees. Moreover, in many systems where a more generous benefit is provided if disability is related to duty causes, policemen or firefighters suffering such illnesses as heart disease, hernia, pneumonia, and tuberculosis are classified as duty-disabled. The difference in treatment between the police and fire employment category and other classifications of public employees has been rationalized in terms of the physical demands made upon policemen and firefighters.

Very commonly, the formulas employed to compute benefits payable following disablement are patterned after normal retirement formulas. However, disability formulas often involve additional complexities, primarily since disability retirement benefits are awarded over a much wider range of age and service than normal retirement benefits. Although an employee disabled with a relatively short period of service will probably receive a smaller benefit than one with more service, the differential is often small and occasionally nil. As an example of the latter, some systems give credit for the projected period of service from the disability date to the normal retirement date. Another method, having similar implications for an employee disabled at a relatively young

---

[1] Social Security Administration Research Report No. 15: *State and Local Government Retirement Systems, 1965* and Research Report No. 23: *Retirement Systems for Employees of State and Local Governments, 1966,* and the author's sampling of Canadian systems.

age, provides a disability retirement allowance equal to a flat percentage of salary, regardless of length of service.

The disability benefit provisions of the California Public Employees' Retirement System[2] include an example of the latter approach. The retirement allowance for a disabled employee is generally his final average salary multiplied by 1½ percent for each year of his credited service or 33⅓ percent, whichever is greater. For certain employees with limited service, only the first of these two formulas is used. In no event, however, may the disability benefit exceed the normal retirement allowance the employee would receive if he were to continue to work until age 60 with no change in his final average salary.

The disability benefits provided by the New York State Employees' Retirement System are similar to those in California, but the New York program has one feature which is not available to most California employees. This is the provision for a larger disability benefit if the disablement results from occupational causes. In such a case, a member's benefit is three quarters of his final average salary, decreased by the workmen's compensation payable to him, but increased by an annuity provided by his own accumulated contributions and by any other contributions made on his behalf by his employer under the special "take-home-pay" provisions of the New York law.

Under the New York system, a member must be unable to perform the duties of *his* position to qualify for the disability retirement allowance. This general type of definition covers the majority of public employees in the United States and Canada. A more stringent requirement—the inability to perform the duties of *any* position—is found in California and

---

[2] For illustrative purposes, specific reference will be made in this chapter to the benefit provisions for general employees (other than policemen, firefighters, and other special employees) covered by the California and New York state systems, the two largest nonfederal public employee retirement systems in North America. To augment the descriptions given here as to the California system, it will be helpful to refer to a description of its benefits as distributed to its members, which is reprinted in a somewhat condensed form in Appendix B.

some other systems. Some systems leave the definition of disability to the discretion of the board without further guidelines.

Regardless of the particular definition a system might have for disability, the question of whether or not a member is disabled often remains subject to differing judgments. For this reason, the disability provisions of a system are in many ways the most difficult to administer. If the decision is made by a board also having certain fiscal responsibilities for the system, a balance between respect for the funds of the system and sympathy for the member can be expected. However, if the determination of disability is made by individuals or boards whose primary association is with the membership, with little or no responsibility for the fiscal integrity of the system, overly generous benefits may be awarded. Obviously, the more clearly the definition of the disability is drawn in the governing legislation, the smaller is the problem of administrative leeway in interpretation of the law.

Death Benefits.   Essentially all public employee retirement systems will refund an employee's accumulated contributions upon his death. The payment is made to a beneficiary either named by him or designated in the system's laws and regulations. Although not quite so prevalent as disability benefits, provisions for additional death benefits are widespread. These benefits may take the form either of a lump-sum payment supplementing the member's accumulated contributions or of a monthly retirement allowance to the spouse or other beneficiary of the deceased member.

The lump-sum payment may be strictly related to salary, similar to group life insurance coverage. On the other hand, a significant number of systems provide a lump-sum payment which is related to and often matches the accumulated amount of the employee's contributions at the time of death. In several systems, in lieu of taking a lump-sum payment including the accumulated employee contributions, the beneficiary may elect to receive a monthly benefit.

The provision of a monthly benefit to the beneficiary of a deceased member evolves logically from the normal retirement provisions. As mentioned in the previous chapter, most systems allow a retiring member to choose a reduced monthly amount instead of his regular retirement allowance so that a benefit will continue to his beneficiary following his death. For an employee who is in ill health at the time of retirement, this provision is of substantial value. Many systems recognize this value and make available a modification of the provision prior to retirement. If a member of such a system dies while eligible for normal retirement, his benefit is computed as if he had actually retired. If he had elected an optional benefit to be continued to his beneficiary, payment is made to the beneficiary in accordance with the option. In some systems, the continuation option is automatic when a member dies in such an instance; the beneficiary has the right to monthly payments even if the employee did not elect that option. In such an instance the spouse of the employee is often designated the beneficiary by statute, so that this type of benefit is often called a *spouse's benefit* or *widow's benefit*. The age or service boundary at which the employee becomes eligible for this benefit can prove severe in some instances, causing some systems to extend this provision to members who are not otherwise eligible for normal retirement. In most systems the beneficiary must forgo the lump-sum payment otherwise payable in order to receive the monthly benefit. Since the monthly benefit is related to the total benefit the employee has accrued, it is generally worth considerably more than the lump-sum payment, which usually is merely the employee's contributions accumulated with interest.

The California Public Employees' Retirement System provides examples of many of the forms of death benefit available under public employee systems. The basic death benefit payable in behalf of all active members is a lump sum equal to one month's salary for each year of contributing service, up to a maximum payment of six months' salary. To this is added the member's contributions accumulated with interest. In lieu of this basic death benefit, the beneficiary of an active member who dies after age 55 with 5 years of credited service may choose a monthly allowance of one half of the normal retirement allowance the member would have received had he retired immediately prior to his death. In addition, a death benefit of $500 is provided for retired members.

For members of the California system not covered by social security, an additional survivor benefit is provided. This benefit is similar to the social security family benefit paying specific monthly amounts to widows and dependent widowers, children and parents. This benefit requires from each employee an additional $2 of monthly contributions which cannot be refunded, paralleling the nonrefundability of the social security tax. The coverage was made available in 1959 to many California employees not then covered for social security. Those who chose the California coverage could not later drop it nor could those refusing it later be covered. The coverage has been mandatory for all employees hired more recently into many positions not covered by social security.

There is no benefit under the New York State Employees' Retirement System which compares with the United States social security family benefit program. In other respects, however, there are similarities between the death benefits under the New York and California systems. The lump-sum benefits payable on behalf of deceased members in New York are computed by essentially the same formula as that used by the California system. A benefit is also available to the beneficiary of an employeee who dies while eligible for service retirement. Some aspects of the death benefit provisions are more generous in New York than in California. The usual lump-sum benefit in New York is $20,000 or three times the deceased employee's annual salary, whichever is smaller. In addition, the New York system provides a larger benefit to the beneficiary of an employee who dies from injuries sustained on his job. The beneficiary of such an employee receives a pension equal to one half of the employee's final average salary, reduced by any workmen's compensation payable. In addition, the beneficiary receives a cash payment of the member's accumulated contributions and any employer contributions accumulated in the employee's behalf under the system's "take-home pay" provisions.

Early Retirement. Most retirement systems are oriented to providing a certain level of benefit for employees upon their "normal retirement."[3] While an explicit statement to this effect may not be made, the concept of a date at which a full benefit is available, using the basic retirement formula of the system, is often implied. In some instances, no retirement benefits are available prior to this date except in the event of disability. More commonly, though, provisions are made for early retirement, allowing the employee the right to a reduced benefit commencing prior to the date he would have been eligible for the full retirement allowance.

In most situations, an employee who takes advantage of an early retirement provision will not have earned the full benefit to which he would be entitled at his normal retirement date. Under most early retirement formulas, the benefit he has actually accrued will be further reduced to make the amount payable actuarially equivalent in value to the accrued benefit, the latter value being calculated as if payments were to commence at the date he would first be eligible for normal retirement. For example, under the California system, a man who has accrued a benefit of $100 per month, to start at age 60, would receive only $70.62 per month if he retires at age 55. In some systems the factors used for this reduction are set arbitrarily and are not necessarily tied to the basis adopted by the actuary for valuing the retirement benefits.

Where more precise actuarial equivalents are used, however, the factors for men and women will generally differ. In the example given in the previous paragraph, a woman retiring at age 55 would receive $73.02. It is easy to reach the erroneous conclusion that the woman should get less than the man, rather than more, owing to her expected longer life. However, the relative values of the benefits commencing

---

3 See p. 43.

immediately and those deferred 5 years are what govern. For a woman, with a longer life expectancy, the payment of 5 additional years of benefits does not add as much, proportionately, to the expected total period over which payments will be made as such an addition does for a man. Therefore, the percentage reduction for a woman need not be as large as it is for a man.

To qualify for early retirement benefits, an employee must meet certain requirements as to age, period of service, or both. Common requirements in this respect are age 55 and 25 years of service, but many variations exist. The California system, as an example, makes early retirement available at age 55 for an employee who has 5 years of service. It is important to understand the close relationship that exists between vested benefits (see below) and early retirement benefits. Where both are available to an employee, the two are essentially identical in value so long as the method of calculating the early retirement benefit approximates an actuarial reduction of the accrued benefit. The basic difference is that a vested benefit provides for a deferred commencement of monthly payments while the early retirement benefit provides equivalent, and therefore reduced, monthly payments starting immediately.

Vested Benefits.   Only a very small percentage of employees remain on the payroll of their first employer until they retire. Those who become eligible for participation in the organization's retirement system but terminate employment before becoming eligible for retirement benefits would forfeit any retirement benefits which might have accrued unless a provision is made to avoid the forfeiture. Such a provision is called a vesting provision.

In rare instances vesting will result in an immediate benefit, such as a lump-sum payment of employer contributions in an amount matching the accumulated employee contributions. More commonly the vested benefit is a retirement allowance commencing at the normal retirement date in the amount accrued to the date of severance of service. If the normal retirement benefit is based on final salary at retirement, the vested benefit is generally based on a corresponding final salary determined at the date of termination of employment. To be eligible for a vested benefit, an employee must meet certain requirements as to age, service, or both. For example, an employee must have worked for five years under the California Public Employees' Retirement System to qualify. Under the New York State Employees Retirement System, ten years of service, including five years of membership service, are required before vested benefits are available.

In several provinces of Canada, pension benefit acts are in effect which, among other things, require vesting for employees who are age 45 and have 10 years of service. One significant change has been brought about in the vesting provisions of Canadian plans as a result of this legislation. Where these laws apply, an employee who has qualified for vesting in a contributory plan cannot withdraw his contributions upon termination of employment and thereby forfeit his vested rights. Without this restriction, contributory plans generally have *conditional vesting,* vesting which occurs only if the employee leaves his accumulated contributions with the system at termination of employment. Any measurement of the financial effect of a vesting provision is thus substantially affected by the likelihood of forfeiture of vesting by withdrawal of accumulated contributions.

In this regard, a study made of the United States Civil Service Retirement System showed that over three quarters of those eligible for vesting forfeited their rights to a deferred benefit by withdrawing their contributions upon termination of employment.[4] A large number of these forfeitures were of relatively minor amounts of accrued benefits, since the Civil Service System requires only 5 years of service for vesting. Nevertheless, even among those with 20 years of service, over one third of the terminating employees took their contributions instead of a future benefit. Their proclivity for taking the "bird in the hand" was further shown in a separate study

---

[4] Joseph Krislov, "Forfeiture of Civil Service Retirement Benefits," *Social Security Bulletin* (October 1961) , pp. 18–21.

of the same system which revealed that among the latter group—those with 20 years of service at termination of employment—the value of the pension forfeited by withdrawing contributions was about twice the amount of employee contributions withdrawn.[5]

A form of vesting that is receiving increasing attention involves an employee's transfer from one public employer to another. In states and provinces having conglomerate systems encompassing many public employers, coverage will automatically continue without change if both the old and the new employer are in the system. Even where the employers are in different systems, it is not uncommon for systems within any one state to have reciprocity agreements in effect. Thus, an employee changing his employment and moving between two systems having such an agreement maintains his credits in the original system, regardless of his age and service, provided his contributions are not withdrawn. In systems covering public teachers, similar provisions allow teachers the opportunity to acquire credit in some states' systems for previous service as a teacher in another state.

Most of the reciprocity agreements described above will not provide an employee with retirement benefits comparable to what he would have been granted had all his service been with either system or had the systems been consolidated. Where benefits earned in a previous system are frozen under a reciprocal arrangement, they are commonly based on the final salary of the employee prior to his leaving the system, a salary nearly always lower than his final salary in the system from which he ultimately retires. Thus, an employee tranferring between two systems with identical benefit formulas would have a smaller total benefit than if he had worked entirely in one or the other of the systems. In rare instances steps have been taken to correct this inequity, but the vast majority of reciprocal arrangements suffer the shortcoming illustrated. In a larger sense, this same shortcoming is found

5 Robert J. Myers, "Actuarial Analysis of the Relative Value of Refunds versus Deferred Annuities under the Civil Service Retirement System" (Social Security Administration, Actuarial Note No. 2, May 1963) .

in nonreciprocal situations, where an employee's benefits at retirement become the sum of two or more independently earned vested benefits, only the last of which reflects his true final salary.[6]

A similar problem arises where a benefit formula has a graduated feature. For example, one type of benefit formula provides 1 percent of final salary for the first ten years of service, 1.5 percent of final salary for the next ten years, and 2 percent for the balance. If an employee has broken service with two or three systems having similar programs, his total benefit will always be less than the amount that he would have received had he remained with one system for the entire period.

Various solutions have been proposed for these problems. One is for each system to calculate a benefit according to its own benefit formula, assuming all the employee's service had been in that system. Each system then pays a benefit equal to its calculated total benefit multiplied by the percentage of the employee's total service which was spent in that system. Thus, if the benefit structures of all of the systems are identical, the employee receives as a final benefit the same amount he would have received had he remained with any of the systems for his entire career. Also the cost of the benefits would automatically be apportioned among the systems according to the periods served with each.

An obvious alternative to such an elaborate scheme is the conglomeration of the systems involved so that transfer of employment between the given employers will not require that an employee change from one retirement system to another. A related advantage of conglomeration is that it reduces the likelihood of an employee's retiring with a full benefit under a system designed to allow retirement at a young age, and then earning a second retirement benefit in another system.[7]

---

[6] For an expanded treatment of this question, See Dan M. McGill, *Preservation of Pension Benefit Rights* (Homewood, Ill.: Richard D. Irwin, Inc., 1972), Chapter 7.

[7] See p. 20 for other comments on conglomerate systems.

Termination of Employment without Vesting. Essentially all public employee retirement systems provide for return of an employee's contributions with interest if his employment is terminated before he becomes eligible for a vested benefit.

Occasionally the interest portion is not paid to employees who do not meet certain service requirements. In even rarer instances employee contributions are only partially returned or not returned at all, in accordance with the provisions defining the system's benefit structures.

BENEFIT COMPARISONS

The objective of any retirement program should be to provide benefits which, along with a retiree's other retirement income, will be adequate for his postretirement needs. The key word is "adequate." There is no consensus as to the level which brings about adequacy. Beneficiaries and potential beneficiaries seldom accept existing levels as "adequate," so there is a constant striving to increase the level of benefit. For the employer, a prime consideration is the fiscal requirement the plan will entail. Perhaps the only objective guide available is an analysis of what is being done by other plans of a comparable nature.

The principal element of such an analysis will be a comparison of normal retirement benefits. A complete analysis, however, will also include comparisons of the other forms of benefits discussed earlier in this chapter, and of the provisions for membership qualifications and employeee contributions discussed in Chapter 2. Any comparisons between public employee retirement systems and private plans must be made with proper recognition of the intrinsic differences between the two types of employment. These differences include the lack of federal old-age benefits for many public employees, the limited extent of collective bargaining in public employment, the preponderance and compulsory nature of contributory plans in public systems, the effect of civil service on tenure of employment, the special hazards of firefighting and police work, and the unavailability to public employees of stock options, profit-sharing, and like benefits.

Many other considerations affect benefit comparisons in general. Some benefits are simply not comparable in the same frame of reference. For example, comparisons between benefit formulas involving career average salaries and final salaries are most difficult.[8] The availability of social security is a major factor, and its effect on the total benefit package is difficult to measure in objective terms. A similar complication arises when benefits such as group life insurance and disability income insurance are provided outside the retirement program. The degree to which a benefit is utilized can vary significantly between groups of employees, causing one type of benefit, such as a vested benefit, to be far more valuable in one group than another. Finally the comparisons must be constantly monitored to reflect the ever-changing benefit structures under review. This last comment is particularly true of the comparisons to be made in the balance of this chapter, which were developed from statistics chosen to present a snapshot of benefit status in the mid-1960s. Trends since that time have undoubtedly altered some of the relationships and will continue to do so.

Retirement Benefits. The most obvious feature to compare in pension plans is the amount of benefit paid to a person who is retiring. Unfortunately, it is difficult to make such comparisons on a precise basis, primarily because the benefit amount is the end result of many variables, such as the benefit formula, the salary base from which benefits are calculated, and the eligibility requirements for retirement. Nevertheless, some statistics are available to make a rudimentary comparison.

In 1965, the Social Security Administration made a study of 151 retirement systems covering over three million public employees in the United States, most of whom were also

---

[8] This problem is discussed in some detail and a solution presented in "Pension Formula Summarization: An Emerging Research Technique" by Arnold Strasser, *Monthly Labor Review*, April 1971, pp. 49–56. Other aspects of statistical comparisons of retirement benefits are also discussed in this article.

covered for social security benefits.[9] This study disclosed that the median retirement benefit available from the systems to their participants with 30 years of service and with final salaries in the $300–$500 per month range was 36–38 percent of salary. A study of 50 selected private pension plans for salaried employees in the United States at about the same time[10] showed a median benefit for employees with a $400 monthly salary of $120, or 30 percent of salary. A similar study was made by a leading management consulting firm in 1965, covering 490 companies in 33 major industries in the United States.[11] This study revealed that the median employee at the clerical level received a pension of 32.5 percent of his final salary. Where only contributory plans were considered, the median benefit for the clerical employees was 34.5 percent of salary. In both instances, this was after 35 years of service when a larger benefit would be expected than after 30 years of service. For the salary and service range covered, then, it appears that a somewhat larger benefit is paid to a public employee upon retirement than to his private counterpart.[12]

The results are much more conclusive when the comparison includes retirement systems for those United States public employees not covered for old-age benefits under social security. Under the governing federal statutes, political units have the option of choosing social security coverage or not, including the option to terminate coverage once it has been elected. A survey by the U.S. Census Bureau in 1967 indicated that approximately 4.4 million out of a total of 7.1 million employees of state and local governments, or about

---

9 Social Security Administration Research Report No. 15: *State and Local Government Retirement Systems, 1965.*

10 United States Bureau of Labor Statistics, *Bulletin No. 1477, Digest of 50 Selected Pension Plans for Salaried Employees,* Summer 1965.

11 McKinsey and Company, Inc., *Corporate Retirement Programs* (1965).

12 It should be emphasized that only benefits are being compared, not the relative generosity of the employers. If the latter were considered, one of the factors that would have to be weighed is the fact that nearly all public employee retirement systems are contributory, while the employer pays all the cost in most private plans in the United States. The wage levels may also be different.

five of every eight employees, were then covered by the federal Social Security Act.[13]

A study by the Social Security Administration of public employee retirement systems covering employees who were mostly ineligible to accrue social security benefits[14] indicated a level of benefits under these systems significantly higher than the benefits under systems for employees having social security coverage. The range of median benefits for public employees in groups excluded from social security, including policemen and firefighters, was 54–58 percent of final compensation. The corresponding range given earlier for groups largely covered by social security was 36–38 percent. Although the employees in the former category (and their employers) are saved the expense of meeting the social security payroll tax during their public employment, they are also prevented from earning the corresponding social security benefits. For the typical employee at this salary level, the old-age benefits under social security would exceed the differences in the medians given—if retirement occurs at age 65. However, social security benefits are not available at age 60 or earlier, when most policemen and firefighters are eligible for normal retirement. A further complication in such a comparison of benefits is the significant percentage of public employees who gain social security coverage by means of a second job occurring concurrently with their public employment (moonlighting) or after retirement from public service.[15]

Comparable figures are not available for the Canadian private sector. However, based on a sampling conducted by the author, Canadian public employees accrue a significantly

---

[13] U.S. Census of Governments, *Compendium of Public Employment*, Vol. III, No. 2, 1967, Table 10.

[14] Social Security Administration Research Report No. 23: *Retirement Systems for Employees of State and Local Governments, 1966.*

[15] A 1971 survey showed persons whose primary employment was in state and local public administration to have the highest multiple jobholding rate (two or more jobs) of all the industry groups classified. United States Bureau of Labor Statistics, *Multiple Jobholding in 1970 and 1971; Special Labor Force Report 139,* 1972.

higher level of benefits under their retirement systems than is provided in the United States. The median benefits in Canada comparable to the figures given earlier in this section are about 60 percent of final salary.

Disability Benefits.   In contrast to the nearly universal availability of disability benefits in public employee retirement systems, about one third of the group of 490 corporate pension plans surveyed in 1965 did not provide this benefit. The separate study of 50 very large private plans showed more than one fourth of the plans without disability benefits, tending to substantiate the discrepancy between public and private plans. Moreover, this latter study showed that where disability coverage was provided in the private plans, a longer period of service usually was required before an employee was protected than was the case for employees of public systems. For example, only 22 percent of the 50 private plans provided disability benefits when a 25-year-old entrant reaches 35, compared with a coverage of more than 80 percent of the corresponding public employees. In all instances, these comparisons are of the retirement programs themselves, and do not take account of any disability benefits provided by separate insurance arrangements.

Survivors' Benefits.   The difference between private and public employee systems is even more pronounced in the area of monthly benefits for surviving dependents of active employees. The survey of 490 private plans indicated that less than 15 percent of the plans provided some form of monthly pension to the surviving dependent of a deceased employee. Similarly, of the 50 large corporate plans in the separate study, only 24 percent offered this type of benefit.

On the other hand, provision for monthly allowances to beneficiaries of deceased employees is widespread among public employee retirement systems in the United States and Canada. More than 70 percent of the participants in such systems are in systems providing benefits in the form of monthly payments to the survivors of active employees. However, the age and service requirements to be met as a condition of payment of such benefits are substantially less stringent among employees not covered by social security. Thus, while only about 10 percent of the public employees in the United States who are covered by social security and have 15 years of service are also eligible for survivors' benefits under their own systems, those who are not covered by social security are almost universally provided survivors' protection under their systems after that much service. This same high level of protection is also provided for Canadian public employees.

Vested Benefits. Although a large majority of public employees are in systems which provide for vesting prior to normal retirement if age and service requirements are met, a relatively low percentage of police and fire retirement systems offer this coverage. Specifically, less than 40 percent of the policemen and firefighters in the United States and Canada are in systems providing vested rights prior to normal retirement. In contrast, over 70 percent of all other public employees qualify for vested benefits after 20 years of service, the figure rising about 85 percent with 25 years of service. It is difficult to pinpoint the reasons for this distinction, but certainly a primary one is the career concept inherent in the work of a policeman or firefighter. Career-oriented employee groups occasionally object to vesting provisions, contending that vested benefits credited to employees who terminate before retirement are costing the employer money that should be saved and added to the benefits of the employees who remain until normal retirement. This factor, coupled with relatively young retirement ages, may make vesting provisions less important in a system covering police and fire personnel than in one for general employees.

The general subject of vesting and its availability, especially in private plans, has received considerable attention in recent years. A number of legislative proposals in the U.S. Congress have been made which would, in one form or another, establish certain requirements as to vesting for private plans. With this activity as a backdrop, vesting has become increasingly available to employees covered under private pension plans in the United States. Statistics indicating the prevalence of vesting are somewhat incomplete, but those available appear to indicate that private plans have caught up with and passed public employee retirement systems, which had a substantial head start in this respect. As an indication of this, Table 3 provides a comparison of statistics

TABLE 3
Employees Eligible for Full Vesting, Mid-1960s

	Years of Service	
	10	*20*
U.S.: Public Systems	35%	77%
Private Plans	47	81
Canada: Public Systems	60	70
Private Plans	35	85

Source: Public Systems: Social Security Administration Research Reports No. 15 and No. 23. These figures assume employees enter service at age 30.

U.S. Private Plans: Griffin & Trowbridge, *Status of Funding under Private Pension Funds* (Homewood, Ill.: Richard D. Irwin, Inc., 1969), Table 3–8. These figures may overstate the availability of vesting somewhat, since joint labor-management plans with less prevalent vesting are underrepresented.

Canadian Private Plans: Estimated from *Survey of Pension Plan Coverage,* 1965. Dominion Bureau of Statisics, Ottawa, 1967.

from various sources. The figures given in this table for Canada are probably low, particularly in the area of private plans. This is because they were largely based upon statistics gathered before the full effect was felt of recent provincial legislation imposing mandatory vesting provisions.

Chapter 5

Financing—Measuring the Cost

MEASUREMENT of costs is usually the responsibility of an accountant. The measurement of pension costs poses special problems, owing both to the complexity of the issues involved and to the necessity for employing another professional skill, that of an actuary, in arriving at meaningful results. Despite these problems, the accounting profession has developed measurement principles which accountants have applied throughout the private sector. In general, the use of these principles has led to a recognition, during the working lifetimes of the employees, of the cost of providing them pensions after retirement.[1]

---

[1] See Accounting Principles Board of the American Institute of Certified Public Accountants, *Accounting for the Cost of Pension Plans* (New York, 1966). A portion of that opinion, which is often referred to as *APB #8,* states: "To be acceptable for determining cost for accounting purposes, an actuarial cost method should be rational and systematic and should be consistently applied so that it results in a reasonable measure of pension cost from year to year. . . . Each of the actuarial cost methods described in [this *Opinion*] . . . except terminal funding, is considered acceptable when the actuarial assumptions are reasonable and when the method is applied in conformity with the other conclusions of this *Opinion.* The terminal funding method is not acceptable because it does not recognize pension cost prior to retirement of employees. For the same reason, the pay-as-you-go method (which is not an actuarial cost method) is not acceptable."

Adoption of appropriate cost measurement techniques is a logical prerequisite to the development of sound policy for the financing of retirement programs, whether public or private. It is unfortunate, then, that legislators must make decisions regarding the financing of public systems without a consensus comparable to the cost-measurement principles used by the accountants. This is all the more regrettable since most of the considerations applicable in the private sector are equally valid with respect to public systems.

Taxpayers and their leaders in the legislative councils cannot shirk their ultimate responsibilities for the financial functioning of the retirement systems under their jurisdiction. In particular, it is the fundamental duty of the lawmakers to *know* the nature and amounts of the costs of these systems. The purpose of this chapter is to help provide this knowledge by describing the ways pension costs are measured. Chapter 6 will take up the methods employers use to meet these costs.

THREE WAYS TO MEASURE PENSION COSTS

It is just as vital that the persons responsible for a retirement system be aware of its costs as it is that the managers of any other enterprise know the costs associated with it. Unfortunately, however, accounting for the cost of a retirement system is more complex than accounting for most other fiscal functions. The cost of fire protection service, for example, can be measured by adding such expenses as the payroll of the firefighters, the cost of gasoline used, maintenance and depreciation of the firefighting equipment, and rent or depreciation on the fire stations. Most of these items involve current expenditures, which are easily measured. Even the noncash items like depreciation are subject to generally accepted methods that allow the total departmental costs to be easily understood.

Not so in retirement systems. Current disbursements for a retirement system are primarily payments of pensions and other benefits. Although any year's payout measures the cash drain of a system, the payout does not measure the cost. The payout is controlled by events which took place many years earlier. Payment may be continuing to a person long retired. The amount of benefit may have been determined by the pensioner's earnings during a working career which commenced 40 years ago. In a sense, money paid out in any year may be thought of as applying to the operations of a period a generation or more earlier. This basic peculiarity of pension costs points up the desirability of clearly distinguishing the purposes and limitations of the various ways of thinking about cost, especially the ways of assigning costs to specific time periods.

Current Disbursements.   The simplest method of measuring the cost of a retirement system is to add up all of the checks being drawn on it for the credit of its participants and their beneficiaries. Some of these checks are payment for normal retirement, disability retirement, early retirement, and survivors' benefits. Others are payments to terminating employees of their accumulated contributions. Measurement of current disbursements can be in terms of the total payout, or in terms of the net current payout from employer funds. The latter is the excess, if any, of the system's total payout in any period over its income from employee contributions during the same period.

Another way of determining the net employer payout recognizes the special nature of employee contributions. In many systems, money contributed by employees is effectively held in trust for them, generally in the form of investments. The amount set aside for an employee is not released until it is used for a benefit in his behalf or returned to him upon his termination. In this context, the employer commitment can be thought of as being unaffected by current employee contributions or their withdrawal. Instead, under this version of the current disbursement method, the net employer cost is taken as the gross employer payout for retirement allowances less the portion of these allowances derived from employee contributions.

Projections. A major shortcoming of the current disbursement method of cost measurement is that significant changes in the pattern of payments may be impending without being reflected in current payout. Common causes of this adverse characteristic include benefit improvements, changing employment patterns, and salary adjustments. As a result, the finances of a retirement system cannot be properly managed without some method of forecasting future disbursements.

Forecasting methods normally involve the application of the laws of probability to the events to be forecast. Each employee's prospects of receiving various benefits are weighed. For example, based upon the experience of similar employees in the past, a young employee might have a small chance of continuing to retirement. The most likely change of employment status for such an employee is termination prior to retirement, although the chances of disablement or death must also be reckoned with. Attached to most contingencies is a payment or a stream of payments from the funds of the retirement system to the employee or his beneficiary. For each employee, then, probabilities are assigned to each of the possible occurrences which could cause payments to be made each year in the future. Where these payments are to continue on a monthly payment basis, such as after normal retirement, projection of the monthly payments for their expected duration is carried out by the further application of probabilities.

This process is unreal when applied to only one individual. While probabilities are given in fractions which assess the fractional likelihood of specific occurrences coming to pass, the individual's actual experience will take only one of the many available courses to the exclusion of all others. For this reason, the statistical techniques used in projections are more meaningful when applied to a group of people. The larger the group, the more precise the prediction, provided the underlying probabilities assumed for the predictions are correct. These probabilities are called *actuarial assumptions*.

The considerations which affect the choice of actuarial assumptions will be discussed later in this chapter.

The mechanics of cost projections can involve substantial labor. The computer is ideally suited to take over the arduous calculations formerly carried out by hand. As a consequence, the projection technique for measuring cost will continue to grow in usage.

Actuarial Cost Method. The current disbursement method reflects the cost of a payment in the year in which it comes due. A projection does the same, but anticipates future payments by forecasting them. The next step beyond such a forecast is an *actuarial cost method,* which creates an *equivalent* cost that does not need to occur at the same time as the actual payment. As a simple example, monthly payments involved in an installment purchase can be converted to a single equivalent cost at the time of purchase by applying interest discounts to the future payments. Although most applications of actuarial cost methods are more complex than this, the principle is the same. In essence, the difference between a projection and an actuarial cost method is simply the interest assumed to accrue between the incidence of the equivalent actuarial costs and the corresponding projected benefit disbursements.

One of the basic tools in actuarial cost methods is the *present value.* In general terms, this is defined at some point in time as the single amount equivalent to a payment or series of payments at some future time. For example, suppose the present value of a person's retirement allowance is evaluated at the time of his retirement. The calculation of the present value is based on an actuary's assumptions as to the life expectancy of the retiring person and the rate of interest to be accrued during that life expectancy. In more precise terms, consider a large number of persons retiring on the same day. If the sum of the present values of their allowances were deposited in a bank, the deposit would be exactly sufficient to allow withdrawal of all retirement allowances when they become due. Upon the death of the last pensioner, the account would be completely exhausted, provided the bank regularly credited the rate of interest the actuary assumed and the life expectancies of the members of the group conformed to the actuary's predictions.

The same concept holds when one series of payments is being converted to an equivalent second set. Suppose an employee's benefits after retirement are equated to a series of level annual installments during his working career and the amount of the annual installment is to be determined. This type of equivalence is used in the projected benefit cost method described later in this chapter. The unknown monthly amount is determined algebraically to be sufficient to build a fund which would last for the life expectancy of the person after he retires. In this calculation, interest is assumed to be credited on the fund balance from the time the annual payments start until the entire fund is exhausted by the payment of retirement benefits.

TWO ACTUARIAL COST METHODS

Techniques used to obtain costs equivalent to the projected benefit disbursements are called actuarial cost methods because the measuring process must be carried out by an actuary, or at least by someone using actuarial techniques. Actuarial techniques are used to assign probable values during an employee's lifetime to the payment of retirement and other benefits on his behalf.

Actuarial cost methods take many forms, the differences resulting from the different purposes of the methods. As an aid to understanding these purposes and the methods themselves, two of the very common methods will be described.[2] These two methods have the common characteristic of allocating the cost of retirement benefits for an employee to the period of time in which the right to receive those benefits is being earned.

---

[2] For a more comprehensive review of actuarial cost methods, see Dan M. McGill, *The Fundamentals of Private Pensions*, rev. ed. (Homewood, Ill.: Richard D. Irwin, Inc.) , Chaps. 7 and 8.

Accrued Benefit Method (Unit Credit).[3]   In the accrued benefit method, the retirement benefit is thought of as being apportioned into segments according to when the employee receives credit for the benefit. The cost of each segment is likewise assigned to the year in which the benefit is credited. The cost is the present value of a retirement allowance whose commencement is deferred until the employee's expected retirement. Normal retirement will usually not be a certainty, owing to the possibility of an intervening disablement, death, or other termination of employment. These contingencies are recognized and their effect reflected in the present value of the normal retirement benefit. For each of these occurrences which can also give rise to some form of benefit payment, a similar process is required in order to measure the total benefit cost of the program. Thus, each possible benefit will be apportioned to the years in which it is earned and the cost of each portion calculated. For any employee, then, a year's total cost under the accrued benefit method is the value of the normal retirement benefit segment credited during that year, plus the cost of any other benefits credited during the year. The employer's total cost, generally called the *normal cost,* is the sum of the year's cost for all employees reduced by any portion of that cost borne by the employees through their contributions.

Some forms of benefits are not easily allocated to the years in which they were credited. For example, in many systems a policeman or a firefighter eligible for normal retirement will receive a benefit equal to half salary, regardless of how many years he works. Since the accrued benefit method measures costs for an employee while he is still active and before the date he will retire has been determined with certainty, the crediting of a portion of such a retirement benefit in any year

---

[3] Many of the actuarial cost methods in common use have two or more names. The names used in this book are those recommended by the Committee on Pension and Profit Sharing Terminology, a unit formed by the Pension Research Council and the Committee on Insurance Terminology of the American Risk and Insurance Association to attempt to set a standard for usage. Reference will also be made, however, to essentially equivalent alternate terms in common use.

is done somewhat arbitrarily. If the entire basic benefit structure of a system is of such a nature, this method of cost measurement might not be as appropriate as a projected benefit method, which is described in the next section.

In defining the amount of benefit payable under various circumstances, most public employee retirement systems give credit for service rendered by an employee prior to the establishment of the system. Accordingly, at the establishment of a system a *supplemental cost* for such prior service may be calculated. This is generally done under all actuarial methods of measuring cost, although the techniques for determining the supplemental cost and its scope vary by the method used. For the accrued benefit method, the supplemental cost equals the present value, as of the date the system is established, of all benefits credited for service prior to that date. Sometimes this is called the *prior service cost*. Although this term is quite descriptive for the accrued benefit method, it does not easily translate to other actuarial cost methods and, in fact, can create misunderstanding in some cases.

The accrued benefit cost method is so named because it measures the cost of benefits as they are credited to the employee. In other words, under this method the employer costs for all benefits accrued to any date will have been recognized by that date either as normal costs or as a supplemental cost. The accrued benefit cost method can therefore be readily used in measuring the cash value of benefits which have vested.

Projected Benefit Method with Supplemental Cost (Entry Age Normal). Another actuarial cost method widely used for measuring the costs of a program of retirement benefits is the projected benefit method. Its concept is simple: A level annual employer cost, the normal cost, is established for each employee. This amount is considered to accrue annually from his employment until his termination of active service. In the aggregate, the normal costs are set at a level such that their accumulations will be equivalent to the projected disbursements on behalf of the covered employees as estimated by actuarial methods. The normal costs may be level dollar amounts or they may be level percentages of payroll.

In some variations of this method, the normal cost is calculated from the date of establishment of a system for each person who is then an employee. This results in high normal costs for older employees, especially if benefits are provided for service prior to the date the system was established. The more common procedure is to calculate the normal cost as a level rate from date of employment as if there had always been a system. This procedure necessitates the calculation of a supplemental cost as a measure of the accumulation of normal costs which would have accrued prior to the establishment of the system.

There is an important difference between the supplemental costs calculated under this method and under the accrued benefit method. Under the accrued benefit method, the supplemental cost is affected solely by the level of benefits credited prior to the date the system was established. Under the projected benefit method, the supplemental cost is affected both by the commitments for prior service and by the leveling of normal costs inherent in this method. The latter factor merits further discussion.

Under the accrued benefit method, the employer normal costs for an employee tend to increase as the employee becomes older. This is primarily due to the effects of interest (the time for payment of benefits is coming closer), mortality (the chance of forfeiting benefits by death is lessening), salary growth (more benefit is earned by the older employee), and turnover (the older employee is more likely to stay on the job to receive his retirement allowance). The projected benefit cost method, on the other hand, is designed to produce a level normal cost rate. This rate must be equivalent to the aggregate of all normal costs under the accrued benefit method since both of these are actuarially equivalent to the ultimate disbursements anticipated, after allowing for interest, mortality, salary growth, and turnover. The normal costs under the accrued benefit method will thus be lower in the earlier years of an employee's working career than those under the projected benefit method and higher as he nears retirement. The supplemental cost under either method is an actuarial accumulation of these normal costs from the date an employee is hired to the date the system is established. Therefore, the accrued benefit method, with lower normal costs in the early years of employment than the projected benefit method, will have a lower supplemental cost.

The two actuarial cost methods have another important difference. The normal cost for any one year under the accrued benefit method is affected by the average attained age of the employees. The normal cost of a group of young employees is lower than that for a group of older employees. The cost pattern may vary from year to year as the age composition of the group varies. Moreover, for a group with no turnover, the normal costs will tend to increase. Under the projected benefit method, on the other hand, the normal cost is designed to be level, so that a stable group produces a stable cost. Even for a group with rates of turnover that vary from year to year, the annual costs will tend to be level. In fact, if the average age of a group of new employees is about the same as the average entry age of all the participants of the system or of the terminating employees the group is replacing, the normal cost should remain constant. Although this rarely occurs precisely, the average age of new employees does not usually vary widely, even though the average attained age of the group may change. For this reason, the normal costs tend to remain more nearly level under the projected benefit method than under the accrued benefit method. This characteristic makes the projected benefit method of great value in assessing the long-term costs both of the basic benefits provided by a retirement system and of changes in these benefits.

The projected benefit cost method is actually a family of cost methods. The particular variation described above is in common use and is further identified as of the species having supplemental costs. The family name "projected benefits" distinguishes the method from the accrued benefit cost method. The name is derived from the necessity of projecting the total benefit payable at retirement, including benefits accruing in the future, in order to determine a normal cost under the method. The normal cost rate calculated for a group of new entrants is the present value of all benefits projected to be payable to them or their beneficiaries during their lifetimes, divided by the present value of all the earnings which the employees are projected to receive during their lifetimes. The ratio of these two quantities is the normal cost rate and is the factor applied to future payrolls to calculate the normal cost of the retirement program.

Supplemental Cost. Under either of the actuarial cost methods described, a supplemental cost is created at the establishment of the system if benefits have been credited for earlier service. Supplemental costs can also arise subsequently, often because of a retroactive improvement in benefits. It is immaterial, in this respect, whether the improved benefits are for service before or after the establishment of the system: An additional supplemental cost will be created.

The amount of the supplemental cost will depend upon the cost method being used. In determining the cost of benefit improvements, a formula used to determine the supplemental cost under the projected benefit method can be extended to determine the increment to the supplemental cost under any method. The additional supplemental cost as measured by this formula is the increase in the present value of projected benefits to be paid because of the benefit improvements, less the increase in the present value of future normal costs. The increase in normal cost enters into the formula since an increase in benefits generally improves the benefits payable to currently active employees and therefore increases normal costs. The overall increase in the supplemental cost thus reflects the total increase in employer commitment, but the initial impact of this is reduced by the expected increase in future normal cost payments.

This general formula can also be used with all actuarial methods to determine the initial supplemental cost. The supplemental cost at the outset is the excess of the present value of projected benefits over the present value of all normal costs expected to be charged. In the accrued benefit method, for example, the future normal costs cover all benefits expected to be credited for service after the date the system is established. Thus the supplemental cost is equal to the present value of the balance of the benefits—those credited for service prior to that date. When a change in benefits occurs, the supplemental cost will necessarily be increased by the change in the present value of the benefits and decreased by the change in the present value of the future normal costs, since all previously anticipated benefits have been accounted for in the supplemental cost and the pattern of normal costs earlier established.

Because of its magnitude and its retroactive nature, the supplemental cost is generally not charged to the year in which the system is established. Instead, it is ordinarily amortized over a period of subsequent years, somewhat as if it were a capital item. A justification for this procedure is that a retirement system aids in the recruiting of employees, improves their satisfaction with their work, and is therefore of continuing value after its establishment. Sound benefit design in such a system generally entails the granting of benefits for prior service. The supplemental cost is thus a price to be paid to acquire the system. As such, it may appropriately be amortized over an extended period of time.

A major consideration in choosing the length of the period for spreading the supplemental cost is the effect the period will have on the interest cost. The determination of the supplemental cost, like other actuarial calculations, is pegged at a particular date. This cost increases when measured at subsequent dates because the payments whose value is being estimated are closer to maturity and will not be discounted so heavily. When the cost is spread over a period of years, the charge to any year because of the supplemental cost is called the *annual supplemental cost* and has a principal and interest component. The sum over the years of all the principal components equals the initial supplemental cost. The interest components are determined as if there were an interest-bearing debt, with each year's interest charge being based on the then outstanding balance. The rate of interest is the same as that used in the most recent determination of the present values of benefits associated with the supplemental cost. A perpetual amortization period may be assumed for the supplemental cost, in which case the outstanding balance remains equal to the initial balance and the amount of the annual supplemental cost will be one year's interest on that liability.

There is considerable leeway in determining the length of the amortization period. An argument advanced for relatively short periods (20 to 30 years) is that the advantages of providing prior service benefits wear off as the employees credited with the benefits retire. The periods of remaining service among employees active at the establishment of a system will rarely extend more than 40 years and tend to average less than half of that. At the other extreme is the contention that the supplemental cost should be converted to a level charge in perpetuity, since the supplemental cost is intrinsic to the system itself and not to any group of employees. The perpetual concept has the advantage of avoiding the discontinuity in cost associated with the termination of a finite amortization period.[4]

A compromise between these alternatives which has some of the advantages of both is to use a fixed number of years for the amortization period at the establishment of the system, and to maintain the *same* number of years each year thereafter. For example, if the period chosen were 30 years, each year the annual supplemental cost would be chosen so that maintenance of that level would amortize the *then* unamortized supplemental cost in 30 more years. If nothing occurs to increase the supplemental cost, the annual supplemental cost will gradually decrease under this method but never be completely eliminated. If the supplemental cost should be increased, such as would occur with an increased benefit structure, this method will cause the additional supplemental

---

[4] When used as a basis for meeting the costs of a system, failure to amortize the supplemental cost has important pitfalls. See p. 121.

cost to be amortized at the same rate as was the initial supplemental cost.

ACTUARIAL ASSUMPTIONS

If either projection techniques or actuarial cost methods are used, predictions of future events must be made. These predictions should be made by a competent actuary. They evolve from the compounding of probabilities or assumed rates of occurrence of certain types of events. The primary elements in the process are called actuarial assumptions and involve predicting rates of:

Termination from employment
Disablement
Retirement
Death
Salary increase
Postretirement adjustment
Investment yield
Administrative expense

Obviously it is to the retirement system's advantage to have the prediction of the costs of the system as nearly correct as possible. Thus, the actuarial assumptions used in making predictions must be chosen skillfully. If the data derived from the system's own experience is insufficient, the system's actuary may have to rely upon similar experience in other employee groups in making his predictions. Where possible, though, he looks to the experience of the system itself in establishing assumptions for the valuation of its costs. In either event he also attempts to spot trends so as to anticipate changes from past experience.

For example, in estimating the rates of future termination from employment, the actuary commonly reviews the experience of the system over a recent period of years and from this experience constructs a table of estimated withdrawal rates. Similarly, if the system provides a benefit based upon salary at the time of retirement, the actuary reviews actual salary increases for the covered employees to aid in estimating future salaries and projecting the benefits payable at retirement. As another example, the yield on the system's investments in the recent past is used as a guide in establishing an assumed rate of interest earnings in the future. In each case, if employment conditions or the general state of the economy warrant it, he modifies the past rates in an attempt to predict future experience more accurately.

Setting the assumed rate of investment earnings poses special problems. A factor tending to complicate the measurement of past yields on a system's funds is the effect of capital gains or losses, both those realized in the sale of securities and those unrealized but recognized in the asset valuation technique being used by the system.[5] If gains and losses are included in the calculations, the yields tend to swing widely from year to year as the market swings, especially in a system having substantial stock investments. Such performance may not be much help in setting the assumptions for future yields, since for practical reasons it will generally be desirable to assume a stable rate or set of rates in the future. In many systems, eliminating capital gains and losses from the calculation does not solve the problem, since they may be the major factor in the long term yields of the system, particularly in those systems with aggressively managed investments. What is often needed is a method of averaging the yields to even out the swings. Techniques for this have been developed primarily as an aid to the investment manager, but they can also be used by the actuary to aid him in setting his assumptions as to future earnings rates. Another helpful procedure is to determine the yields separately for the various investment categories, such as bonds, stocks, and mortgages. This serves as a guide for investment results by category and facilitates forecasts if a change in investment strategy is contemplated.

Comparisons of yields among systems can be valuable as an indication of relative success in meeting investment goals.

---

[5] See p. 125.

Such comparisons can serve as a useful guide to future anticipated investment returns in a specific system. Unfortunately no uniform standard for comparing yields is in use. Comparisons will thus be inexact unless the systems being compared happen to be using the same procedure.

ANALYSIS OF TECHNIQUES OF MEASURING COSTS

The ultimate costs of a retirement system will be fixed as its actual expenditures emerge and are measured by the current disbursement method. It is important, however, that these costs be estimated in advance to measure the employer's commitment under the system. The two basic methods for doing this have been described earlier in this chapter. One way is by using projections. Another approach is to determine equivalent costs prior to the actual disbursements. These equivalent costs can then be used either to associate costs with the period in which the rights to benefits are acquired or to measure the relative expense of possible changes in the benefit structure. These general comments will serve to introduce a more detailed analysis and comparison of the cost measuring techniques.

Current Disbursement Method.   The current disbursement method has one major advantage—simplicity. It is easily understood and there is no ambiguity about its results. Unfortunately, it also has a number of disadvantages. It fails to assign the cost of a retirement program to the time an employee is at work, when all other payroll costs are being accounted for. It measures the effects of events which occurred many years ago and are beyond the control of the present generation. It is therefore a very remote and insensitive measure of benefit changes and employment conditions of the present. Over an extended period, costs measured by this method tend to increase as the size of the retirement benefit payroll grows. In the short run, current disbursement costs are subject to substantial fluctuations, as active employees sporadically retire or retired employees die. In short, the current disbursement method is like a house thermometer read once a month: The results may be of interest, but the instrument used this way would hardly serve as an effective thermostat for regulating the furnace.

Projections.   Probably no other actuarial technique is as meaningful to a layman as a projection. The final figures can be checked against actual results, at least in the short run, and this reinforces the understanding of the process. In a well designed and documented projection, the cost segments are sufficiently isolated that the skilled observer may test the reasonableness of the results. In like manner, if adequate detail is provided, the yearly progression of figures will illustrate the usual growth in benefit payments, whereas a single, long-term projection of the final amount might lack credibility.

A major disadvantage of any projection is its reliance upon statistical techniques. Time may prove the projection wrong, due to random variations in experience or because of inaccurate assumptions as to the underlying probabilities of future mortality, disability, rate of employment termination, and the like. For whatever reason, any inaccuracies in a prediction tend to diminish the acceptance of subsequent ones.

Actuarial Cost Methods in General.   Actuarial cost methods are also afflicted with the disadvantages of inaccurate predictions. In addition, the nontechnical observer can find them complicated and difficult to understand. This is aggravated by the lack of a consensus as to a single proper actuarial cost method. There are several major types of methods used and many variations within each type. The distinctions between the variations generally arise for valid reasons. Nevertheless, even specialists in the retirement area, including actuaries, find it difficult to grasp the implications of all the actuarial methods to which they are exposed. It is not surprising, then, that confusion is easily bred in this respect among novices in the field.

Offsetting these disadvantages are many favorable features.

Actuarial cost methods assign the costs of a retirement program to the time an employee is at work, when all other payroll costs are being accounted for. They give a current measure of current changes in benefits or experience. They tend to be relatively stable. They readily put a price on the establishment of a retirement system and distinguish that cost from costs that arise after the system is in operation. They measure costs in today's dollars rather than in dollars payable at some time in the future. In short, actuarial cost methods are indispensable in the proper financial management of a retirement system.

Differences in Actuarial Cost Methods.   Between the two actuarial cost methods described earlier in this chapter, there are certain distinctions to be noted. The accrued benefit method identifies the costs associated with benefits credited to any date. In the same manner, it identifies the costs of benefits earned in any year. It is therefore a valuable measure of benefits earned if a cash equivalent is to be offered to a terminating employee. On the other hand, the projected benefit method avoids the portrayal of increasing costs which generally are associated with the accrued benefit method.

Also, the projected benefit method is inherently superior in giving full recognition to benefits expected to be credited during an employee's working career, thereby avoiding deferred increases in cost and offering the best method of measuring the costs of benefit improvements. Moreover, its level cost characteristics make it the easiest to relate to payroll as a measure of the overall fiscal impact of a retirement program. Level costs simplify the comparison of one benefit structure with another.

COST COMPARISONS

Comparisons are commonly made of the costs of different benefit structures, either within a system or among systems. In general terms, where benefits are greater, costs are greater. Broad conclusions in the area of cost comparisons can thus be based on benefit comparisons. The analysis of differences in benefit structures summarized in the previous chapter may help in making overall cost comparisons among public employee retirement systems and private plans.

The uses of cost comparisons are not limited to analyzing the benefit structures of two or more systems. Comparisons can be used to put a price on a change in the benefit structure within a given system. Such a process really involves a comparison of the costs of the existing benefit program with those of the new program, a simpler procedure than a comparison of costs between two systems.

In the ideal situation, the comparison of a particular benefit feature between two systems is made with all other factors identical. In practice, factors tend to be different rather than identical, making analysis of cost differences difficult. In addition to benefit differences, cost comparisons are affected by the cost methods being used, the actuarial assumptions, the effect of the benefit programs on termination of employment, the distributions of employees by age and service, and any number of other factors. The rest of this chapter deals with some of the factors whose cost implications are more obscure.

Cost Method.   Fundamental to any cost comparison is the cost method being used. It is the yardstick used for the measurements. Substantial differences in cost may appear to exist solely because of differences in cost methods. It is nearly impossible to reach meaningful conclusions in an analysis of cost differentials in two systems if they employ different cost methods.

Even if the same cost method is used, comparisons can be difficult. For example, the current disbursement method will not display many of the effects of a simple benefit increase for many years. On the other hand, an actuarial cost method will give immediate recognition to such benefit changes. In fact, the current disbursement method is unresponsive to projected benefit changes for active employees. For this reason, this method is unsatisfactory for comparing the benefit structures of different systems. A projection may not be much better because of the difficulty of comparing a varying series of numbers.

When certain types of deferred benefits are compared, the projected benefit cost method is superior to the accrued benefit method. For example, suppose a plan with a benefit formula providing 1.5 percent of final salary for each year of service is compared with one providing 1 percent for each of the first ten years, 1.5 percent for the next ten, and 2 percent for the remainder. For various employees, the first plan would appear to be more costly, identical in cost, or less costly by the accrued benefit method, depending on the service of the employees at the time the cost is measured. The projected benefit method overcomes this anomaly by, in effect, merging the cost elements of the latter formula into an equivalent single rate. This rate can then be more readily compared with the rate appropriate to the level formula.

In general, cost comparisons using the projected benefit method are the most precise in establishing an immediate distinction between benefit features whose costs ultimately emerge under the other methods. The accrued benefit method ranks closely behind the projected benefit method in this characteristic, with the current disbursement method far behind. Although a projection improves on the current disbursement method, the projected results may be difficult to interpret because of variations in cost occurring over a long period of time. The ability of a cost method to respond promptly to the cost elements of benefits is obviously of basic importance in making cost comparisons, including those made to evaluate an improvement in benefits. For that reason, it is almost a prerequisite to a significant cost comparison that an actuarial cost method, and in some cases the projected benefit cost method, be used.

Actuarial Assumptions. The major area of uncertainty in the use of a projection or an actuarial cost method involves the choice of actuarial assumptions. If the assumed rates predict the future perfectly, the numbers produced are perfect measures of the costs of the system. Since the assumed rates are, instead, only approximate, so also are the costs they project. The foregoing is essentially obvious. What is not so obvious is the effect the assumptions have on cost comparisons.

Just as the costs for a system will appear to change when a different cost method is used, so also will the costs appear to change when different assumptions are used. The difference in the first case is the result of measuring different costs—current outgo instead of anticipated outgo, for example. The difference in the second case results from actual error and, if the error is significant, any comparison using the erroneous costs will suffer accordingly. This is particularly important in comparing the costs of two systems where the actuarial assumptions used for one are significantly more accurate than those used for the other. The resulting comparison may be misleading. Ideally a comparison should be made using assumptions as close to reality as possible. Lacking this it is sometimes preferable to recalculate costs for one or both systems to get them on a comparable basis, even though the absolute level of costs so measured for each system may not be any more precise. This latter approach may give poor figures as to the absolute level of costs, but the errors may be cancelled when the relative costs for the two systems are compared.

Employment Characteristics. In any comparison of costs, attention must be paid to the characteristics of employment inherent to the groups of covered employees. This is especially important if the comparison involves classifications of public employees whose unique types of work create unusual work patterns. A good example is the category of policemen and firefighters. One of the most notable of the characteristics setting them apart from other employees is their tendency to retire at an early age. This, coupled with their relatively low turnover rates and high disability rates, makes their cost characteristics unusually high.

Examples of a similar nature are found in other job classifications. In some areas of public employment, such as in the legislature or the judiciary, participants in retirement systems will be enrolled at ages which are higher than the average. This results in a cost, as measured by an actuarial cost method, which is substantially higher than that associated with the hiring of younger employees. The effects of interest and employee turnover on actuarial costs are primarily responsible for this higher cost. The employee hired at an advanced age is more likely to continue in service to retirement. The benefits he earns are paid sooner, so that the interest discount on the payments to be made following retirement is correspondingly less than would apply to an employee hired at a younger age.

A similar high cost factor is found in the unusual pattern of employment which typifies some women teachers. They work for a few years following graduation from college, marry and raise families, and then return to work when the children are grown. In many respects, particularly if the credit for earlier service is lost, this pattern of employment has cost effects similar to those of employees hired at a late age.

Rate of salary growth also has an important cost effect. In some occupations the peak salary is often reached fairly promptly after commencement of work, with a very flat growth in salary thereafter, except as caused by inflation. For reasons similar to those causing low costs for employees hired at an early age, employees having these relatively small increases of wages will tend to have lower retirement costs, when measured against their total earnings, than those with sharply increasing salaries.

Requirements for Employee Participation.   Differences in the age or service requirements for participation in systems can give rise to apparent cost differences which may prove to be illusory. A high rate of cost, expressed as a percentage of the salaries of covered employees, may occur for a system having restrictive eligibility requirements. If the cost of this system were spread over the entire payroll, including salaries for those not yet eligible for participation, the resulting rate might prove more reasonable. This latter rate would probably be a better basis for a comparison with a system without such membership restrictions.

Consideration should also be given to the effect on benefits of the waiting period required before an employee can participate in a system. If this preparticipation period is not given credit in determining benefits, an employee in a system with more restrictive eligibility requirements will tend to get lower benefits than an employee in a system with immediate participation. If the systems are noncontributory, the total employer costs will be proportionately lower in the system with delayed eligibility. The same will be true in those contributory systems where the employee's contributions are converted to annuities at retirement to supplement the employer-bought pensions. In many contributory systems, however, the total retirement allowance is on a scheduled basis and the employee contributions are merged with the employer money to provide this benefit. In these cases, the employee contributions in the first year or two of employment can be more than enough to pay for the benefit credited during that time. In such an instance, the total employer cost would actually be reduced by eliminating the eligibility period and providing for immediate participation. In other words, in this type of situation the additional benefits created by eliminating the waiting period would be more than paid for by the additional employee contributions.

Employee Contributions.   For a system providing a given level of retirement allowance, employee contributions result in an obvious reduction in the total employer financial commitment. This is of major significance in public employee retirement systems, nearly all of which are contributory. It is of even greater importance in comparisons with private plans in the United States, where noncontributory private plans predominate.

The effect of employee contributions on the actual cost of a retirement program can be deceptive. In the absence of full and immediate vesting provisions, contributions by the employer generally buy more retirement benefits than the same amount in employee contributions. When a nonvested employee terminates, his own contributions are nearly always returned to him, usually with interest, whereas any employer contributions on his behalf are released to meet the commitments of the employer to other employees under the system. In this context, the money required to pay the retirement benefits of an employee might be thought of as coming from his own contributions, from the contributions of his employer with respect to him, and also from a portion of the employer's funds released by the nonvested terminations or deaths of other employees during the working career of the retiring employee.

The converse of this concept is worth stating: The level of costs of a particular portion of an existing system, or of a proposed modification in benefits, varies depending upon whether the employer or the employee is to pay the costs. Thus, if a certain benefit has been evaluated in terms of employer contributions, a larger total amount is required if the cost is to be split between the employer and the employees, and an even larger amount is needed if the cost is to be paid solely by the employees. This is because the employee portion will be made in the form of contributions which are returnable in the event the employee terminates or dies. If the same amount at retirement is to be provided as would be available if the employer only were making the contributions, larger contributions must be made by the employees ultimately retiring to make up for those withdrawn by terminating employees.

Normal Retirement Date.   The age at which an employee retires has a most significant effect upon costs, but the measurement of the cost of changing retirement ages is difficult. In the simplest context, consider an employee eligible to retire at age 65. He is now age 60 and the law governing the system has just been changed to allow him to retire immediately and receive his full accrued monthly benefit. If he retires immediately, the monthly benefit payments he can expect to receive before age 65 are about 25 percent of those he would have expected to receive had he accrued no additional benefits, lived to age 65 and then retired. His true gain because of retiring early, however is even greater. He gains an interest advantage by receiving payments immediately. In addition, he has about 1 chance in 12 of dying before age 65, so that planning to defer his retirement until then creates the risk of losing all of his benefits by death. For these reasons, the value of his accrued pension has increased by about 50 percent as a result of his opportunity to retire at age 60.

In the usual circumstance, an employee would be able to accrue additional benefits after age 60 if he continued at work. If the cost effect of a normal retirement date at a younger age is viewed from the point of view of the retirement system, the potential benefit to be earned in the next five years of service has been forfeited by the immediate retirement. Recognition of this might reduce the extra cost of advancing the normal retirement date in the instance cited to a one-third increase, instead of a one-half increase in cost. Similarly, immediate retirement eliminates the cost of death benefits if they are provided only for active members by the system. Also, if the benefit is based upon final salary, the retiring employee forfeits any increase in benefit that would result from future salary increases.

As a further complication, it is not unusual for legislation lowering the age for normal retirement also to increase the amount of benefit which can be accrued at the younger retirement age, to make up for the pension otherwise earned to the later retirement date. If this is the case, the cost of the earlier normal retirement, of course, is further increased. In addition, the younger retiree must be replaced earlier, increasing the employer's expense of training each new employee. In short, the cost implications of an early retirement age are tightly intertwined with practically all the other factors influencing the costs of a retirement system. The specific costs are governed by the conditions surrounding each system. In general, though, it is quite clear that a lower age for normal retirement results in higher costs.

Postretirement Adjustments. The effect of the actuarial assumptions on cost comparisons was discussed earlier in this chapter. Of particular difficulty is the prediction of the factors governing postretirement adjustments, such as changes in the consumer price index or in the salaries of active employees. The difficulty is compounded with earlier normal retirement dates, since early retirement extends the period over which postretirement adjustments operate. For these reasons cost comparisons are particularly difficult if they are of systems with post-retirement adjustment mechanisms related to indexes or salaries.

One adjustment mechanism that is usually an exception to this difficulty is the yield-related adjustment. A common form of yield-related adjustment mechanism is the equity annuity, where the amount of benefit payment rises or falls with the value of a portfolio of common stocks held by the system or on the system's behalf. The employer's cost is essentially unaffected if an equity annuity is used, since the portfolio is considered to be assigned to the retirees and any increases in benefits are covered by (in fact, generated by) increases in the value of the portfolio, and vice versa.[6]

A complicated cost comparison may result if a yield-related form of adjustment is combined with another mechanism. For example, some systems provide that an index-related adjustment will occur only if there are sufficient assets to meet the cost of the increase. If a block of common stocks is allocated to cover the retired life liabilities, this type of mechanism assumes many of the characteristics of an equity annuity. In any event, a cost comparison involving such a system poses special problems.

Vested Benefits. A negative approach may clarify the fiscal effect of vesting. Without vesting, a terminating employee loses the service retirement benefit he has accrued.

---

6 This analysis somewhat oversimplifies the case. In a rising market, the employer's commitments might be thought of as being increased by the existence of the adjustment mechanism, since the capital gains might have been used to reduce the employer's other costs if they were not committed to the increased retirement benefits. The reverse holds true, of course, in a declining market. Another complication arises if mortality assumptions are not sufficiently conservative, resulting in an increased employer cost to pay larger benefits beyond the employee's expected life span.

The value of this accrued benefit is eliminated from the employer's responsibility, thereby reducing his costs. If there is a high rate of employee turnover, repeated releases of the employer's liabilities can account for one third, one half, or even more, of the employer's potential costs. Full, immediate vesting, then, increases the employer's costs by not allowing this release of liability to occur.

Under most public employee retirement systems, an employee will forfeit any vested benefits if he withdraws his accumulated contributions upon termination of employment. This form of vesting is called conditional vesting. The costs normally associated with vested benefits tend to disappear in a system having conditional vesting, since most employees forfeit their vested benefits by withdrawing their contributions.

The effect of vesting on the costs of a pension plan can be substantial. If a cost comparison is made between public and private plans, the question of conditional vesting becomes paramount. As mentioned in the previous chapter, provincial legislation in Canada tends to equalize the cost impact of vesting upon both public and private benefit programs by making vesting mandatory after certain age and service conditions are met and prohibiting the withdrawal of employee contributions when he is eligible for vesting. In the United States, on the other hand, vesting provisions would seem to place more of a cost burden on private plans than on public systems. This is due both to the generous vesting provisions in private plans and to the prevalence of contributory plans with conditional vesting in the public area.

Chapter 6

Financing—Paying the Cost

THE FINANCIAL WORKINGS of a public employee retirement system are generally set in motion for a new employee by his initial contribution to the fund associated with the system. Often this contribution triggers a payment to the fund on the employee's behalf by his employer. As the fund builds up from repetition of this operation for each employee, the money is invested, adding interest and dividends to the flow into the system. In some cases, a portion of the fund is used to pay the expenses of administering and maintaining the system. The final step in the process is the payment of benefits to the participants in the system and their beneficiaries.

The whole fiscal arrangement has been compared to a water network, with the system's funds represented by a reservoir.[1] Inputting to this reservoir are three flows: employee money, employer money, and earnings on the investments of the fund. The outflow is for benefit payments and administrative expenses. So long as the reservoir is not empty, the system will continue to operate. Because the input from employee contributions and investment earnings is not easily

---

[1] Charles L. Trowbridge, "ABC's of Pension Funding," *Harvard Business Review,* Vol. 40, No. 2 (March-April 1966) , pp. 115–26.

altered, proper design of the system requires anticipation of the expected outflow in advance, so that the demands on the employer can be scheduled. This is the essential scope of financing techniques—measuring the anticipated outflow and regulating the rate of input of employer contributions into the fund.

This analogy can be extended to illustrate two methods of financing. At one extreme is the "empty reservoir" approach, where practically no money is accumulated in the fund and the employer contributes only what is necessary to meet the current outflow after allowing for the employee contributions and the minimal investment earnings. Such a method is often referred to as the pay-as-you-go method, or current disbursement approach. Since the benefit flow will tend to increase, this method requires correspondingly increasing employer contributions.

At nearly the other end of the spectrum is a method employing a stable flow of water into the reservoir in an amount exceeding the initial outgo. This fills the reservoir, which serves to bring in a substantial flow from interest earnings and to anticipate the larger demands of later years. This technique and its variations are called funding methods, since they involve the setting aside of significant funds for the payment of future benefits.

The previous chapter was designed to give an understanding of what happens in the important pipes and valves of the system and an appreciation of the differences between the flows at the input and output ducts. In this chapter the discussion will focus on the master valve—the one that regulates employer contributions into the system. As this chapter is read, it will be well to keep in mind the problems that can occur when the watershed is dry and no employer contributions are forthcoming. It will also be advisable to recognize the planning and foresight needed because of the size of the input pipe, which limits the flow of employer contributions. The implications of both an increasing and decreasing community on the workings of the system should also be noted.

The simplistic concepts of the analogy are not adequate,

unfortunately, to encompass the complication of the time factor. Some benefit payments may follow the period of work during which they were earned by half a century or more. This interval tends to dim the sense of responsibility of taxpayers and their legislative representatives for providing the proper employer input into the reservoir. It also introduces an area of uncertainty in the prediction of the outflow from the reservoir many years hence. Despite these handicaps, the system should not be altered nor should a valve be turned without attempting to determine the effect on the total operation, now or in the future. In plain language, responsible management demands that the fiscal implications of the benefit program, or a change in that program, be disclosed to the taxpayers and understood by their representatives.

One final introductory note is in order. A conscious effort has been made in this chapter to present each side of the funding issue impartially, despite a strong conviction of the author that the costs of public employee retirement systems should be met as the benefits are being earned. In other words, the fundamental arguments in favor of funding are more convincing than those against, in the author's opinion.

TO FUND OR NOT TO FUND

The term "funding" is commonly used to denote the practice of building up a fund of money or investments for the purpose of meeting future retirement system obligations. Unfortunately, the definition in this form is not sufficiently limiting to distinguish trivial funding practices from those of some significance. For example, such a definition might cover a scheme whereby sufficient funds are accumulated at the beginning of a biennium to pay all the benefits coming due during the biennium. However, such a procedure has essentially all of the attributes, both good and bad, of a nonfunded program and none of those described later for a funded one.

It might be well to review the reason funding exists at all. Consider, for the moment, the distinction between retirement benefits and most other types of nonsalary benefits such as, say, a group life insurance policy making immediate lump-sum settlements. At the end of any period of time, the benefits granted by such a policy for a group of persons will have been fully paid. If no one died, there is no residual liability; if deaths did occur, payments will have been made to the beneficiaries. At the end of the period no employee has the right to any payments yet to be made. Not so for a retirement plan. If no one has terminated during the period, no benefits will have been paid for the active group, yet each active employee will have been credited with additional benefits. At the end of the period, a liability exists for the ultimate payment of those benefits. As the term will be used in this book, *funding* refers to a systematic program under which assets are set aside in amounts and at times approximately coincident with the accruing of benefit rights. As a by-product of a funding technique, in the example given, funds are on hand at the end of the period in approximately the same amount as the value of the liability for benefits credited since the system was established.

The methods that can be used to measure the costs of retirement systems were discussed in the previous chapter. Two of the methods were called actuarial cost methods. If such methods are used, the costs of a retirement system are assigned to the periods during which the credits for benefits are being granted. If the employer contributions are made to match the costs being incurred, as measured by one of the actuarial cost methods, the system is being funded. Failure to make such employer contributions is a failure to fund. The extreme of nonfunding techniques is for employer contributions to be at just such a level as to meet current payout. This obviously is meeting the costs as measured by the current disbursement method, or "pay-as-you-go" method.

In the next few pages arguments on either side of the funding question will be given. Analysis of these arguments will be simplest in most instances if the current disbursement method is thought of for a nonfunding approach and if one of the actuarial cost methods described in the previous chapter is thought of as the guide to employer contributions under a funded method. The funding methods are identified by the corresponding actuarial cost methods: e.g., the *accrued benefit funding method* or the *projected benefit funding method*.[2]

ARGUMENTS AGAINST FUNDING

Financial Hardship.   At the core of essentially all arguments against funding is the type of financial commitment that funding requires. At the establishment of a system employer contributions are needed for funding, both for benefits credited for earlier service and for current accruals. A funding method requires these employer contributions, even though the need is not evidenced by equal demands for current benefit payments. Likewise, in a system whose active membership is growing, each additional employee generates an additional actuarial cost and thus a need for increased employer contributions, even though the current benefit level may not be growing so rapidly. This results in the allocation of current tax revenues for the purpose of building up a fund that will not be called upon for many years. This is not easily accepted, especially when the competition for the tax dollar is extreme such as during an economic downturn. The legislative body may have to choose between the retirement fund and a relief project. Having both by raising taxes is an alternative not easily chosen. Even if a funded system has been adopted and maintained, it is not immune to efforts to reverse the situation. In fact, the pressures to abandon funding may be intensified by a system that has built up a substantial fund. Continuation of funding will probably result in continued growth of the fund, whereas a nonfunding approach will allow the fund to be drawn upon until ex-

---

2 Only two funding methods are discussed, corresponding to the two cost methods presented in Chapter 5. For ease of description, these methods are referred to by their family names and the technical distinctions within the family are omitted. The correct name of the projected benefit method generally referred to in the text, for example, is the "individual projected benefit funding method with supplemental cost."

hausted, completely eliminating employer contributions for awhile.

Inadequate Investment Return.   The return on invested funds may not be sufficient to make it worthwhile to pay now for future cash needs. Governments have traditionally been borrowers. They need money before tax revenues are available and borrow to obtain it. The interest charges exacted by the lenders for the use of the borrowed money are accepted as a necessary governmental expense. The same economic forces which put a premium on immediate cash militate against the governmental agency becoming the lender (i.e., buying securities) if the investment yield to the agency is near that which the government must pay for its money. In this respect, governmental bodies do not have the same tax incentive for funding their retirement systems that private employers have. In the private sector, interest on a corporation's borrowed money is tax-deductible, while interest income on pension fund investments is tax-free, giving the employer the advantage of leverage if he borrows and invests in his retirement fund. The only comparable leverage in governmental systems stems from the tax-free status of interest on most municipal and state bonds held by private lenders in the United States. This reduces the interest rate the local government must pay on its borrowed money relative to what a private borrower must pay. If governmental systems invest in corporate bonds or stocks and the money for the investments is thought of as being derived from a comparable volume of borrowing at the lower municipal bond rates, there will be a difference in yield favorable to the local government. In the case of investment in stocks, part of the differential must be considered as a premium for the risks taken in buying stocks. In any event, the difference in earnings may not be sufficient to offset the immediate needs of the government for the money it would be investing.

Export of Money.   Another objection raised against funding in a public employee retirement system is that the invested monies tend to flow out of the locality from which they were generated, a phenomenon at odds with most governmental expenditures below the federal level. Although this objection can be met by confining investments to local issues, such a policy carries with it a number of hazards.[3] The objection can be completely met by not funding at all, since the government's money will then flow directly to the retirees when their benefit rights mature.

Inflation.   When public employee retirement systems are funded, present taxpayers must set aside funds for payment to employees and their beneficiaries many years in the future. If present inflationary trends continue, the payments ultimately made will probably have substantially less purchasing power than the same dollars do now. A penny saved may only be a half cent earned by the retiree in terms of today's purchasing power. If there is no funding, payments may be made in cheap dollars when they come due rather than in more expensive dollars now.

Hazards of a Large Fund.   A most salient argument against funding in a public system is advanced by the politically cynical. Funding sets aside assets which can attain very substantial proportions. The temptation such a fund can place before the legislature, particularly when beset by pressures for more benefits on the one hand and severe budget limitations on the other, can lead to procrastination in the carrying out of the legislature's fiscal responsibilities at best, or polititical expedience and extravagance at worst.

Government's Guarantee of Benefit.   An argument widely used for funding in the private sector is that the fund itself provides assurance that accrued benefits will be paid when due if future employer contributions are cut off because of bankruptcy, merger, or the like. In public employee retirement systems, particularly at the state and provincial level, their perpetual life and access to theoretically unlimited taxing power may make unnecessary the protection of the large fund.

Administrative Simplicity.   An unfunded system has substantial administrative advantages. Eliminated are the ex-

---

[3] See p. 136 for arguments against investments in local municipal bonds.

penses of acquiring and maintaining a portfolio of investments. It is also unnecessary to carry out the periodic actuarial valuations required under a funded system for the setting of employer contribution rates. The expenses so eliminated may be a significant portion of the overall cost of the retirement program in a small system.[4]

ARGUMENTS IN FAVOR OF FUNDING

Current Payment for Current Services. One major pitfall for a system which does not fund is that it is prey to the "go now/pay later" tactic, by which the legislative authority can appease public employees by raising benefits without increasing current outlay (and thus taxes) significantly. The converse of this, which might be used by the advocate of funding as a rebuttal to the pay-as-you-go argument, would be about as follows: Sound financing of any retirement system requires that benefits accruing to each member be paid for during his active working lifetime by regular contributions to a retirement fund. Thus, when benefit payments commence at retirement, the money will be on hand to provide such benefits until death. In this way, *the cost of benefits for present active members will be borne by present taxpayers and will not become a liability to future taxpayers.*

A corollary to the foregoing argument is that sound financing, as defined above, carries with it an effective discipline on the legislative authority to know and be prepared to meet the costs of a retirement program or its improvements.

The immediate budgetary effect of funding an increase in benefits, even though the change results in no appreciable increment in benefit payments at the moment, is that the legislature must balance the worth of the increased benefits against the immediately increased outlay. In fact the concept of retirement costs as an integral part of payroll not only emphasizes the source of the liability being incurred by the

---

[4] See Donald A. Woolf, "Funding Pensions for Public Employees," *Public Personnel Review,* Vol. 30, No. 3, July 1969 for an expanded version of this argument and of others given here.

employer but also allows a practical means of allocating retirement costs to the appropriate departments and programs.

This same argument can be expressed in a somewhat different manner. When an employee is credited with a unit of retirement benefit for a year's work, his employer has incurred the liability to pay this benefit when it comes due. The debt may not be as formal as a bond issue incurred to build a bridge, for example, but it has many of the same characteristics. If the government fails to fund the retirement commitment, it has an unfunded debt, just as it does with the bonds. However, there is a fundamental distinction between the two types of borrowing. Borrowing to build a bridge can be justified because the bridge will be utilized during the period of repayment. Borrowing for a retirement program, on the other hand, is borrowing for a current payroll expense. Little, if any, justification can be given the future taxpayer as grounds for his having to pay this debt. The debt is being incurred to pay part of the wages of an employee whose services are currently being rendered and are thus of little or no value to the future taxpayer.

Protection of Employee Rights.   The myriad of local plans, below the state or provincial level, are subject to shrinkage of resources as a result of possible population and industrial changes. When such a shrinkage of available money occurs under a nonfunded plan, the results can be disastrous for employees having vested benefits. A properly funded system is much more likely to be able to weather the storm.

This same argument applies to the larger systems but in an altered context. A shortage of tax resources can occur at the state and provincial levels for different reasons but with the same effect as at the lower levels of government. When this occurs, legislative body may find itself hard pressed to meet the commitments left it by its predecessors. Unlimited taxing power may prove very limited indeed. This issue has been eloquently summed up by Rubin G. Cohn as part of an exhaustive and scholarly study of the legal rights of public employees in the benefits provided by retirement systems:

A vested or contractual right in public pensions depends upon the financial stability of the funds. There is little comfort and less sustenance in a contractual right in a fund which is or may become insolvent because of inadequate financing. State financed funds which are determined to be contractual may in fact create illusory and unenforceable rights under circumstances of financial stress. Given typical constitutional grants of sovereign immunity and the legal impracticability if not impossibility of compelling the legislature to make appropriations, or to grant pensions to qualified annuitants where default is threatened or has occurred, the contract right may turn out to be the stuff of which dreams are made . . . The critical factor is not the legal label which defines the rights, but the extent to which the fund can redeem the statutory promises when they fall due.[5]

Investment Earnings.[6] The assets accumulated in a funded retirement system are generally invested in securities whose yields will help meet the costs of the system. Any costs so met would otherwise have been the responsibility of the taxpayer. Funding a system, then, serves to reduce the taxes that will be required for its maintenance.

The effect of inflation on the funding process deserves further attention. A commitment to pay $1,000 30 years hence can be financed by investing about $250 now at 5 percent interest and letting the investment grow to the $1,000 amount, or it can be financed by waiting 30 years and meeting the obligation at that time. If inflation has reduced the purchasing power of the dollar so that the $1,000 buys, say, only what $500 would buy now, this has, in one sense, reduced the true investment yield earned on the $250 from 5 percent to about 2.5 percent. The lesser rate is still to the employer's advantage, since the investment earnings have reduced the employer's commitment both in dollars and in terms of purchasing power. Investment earnings will continue to do so as long as the yield on investments exceeds the rate of inflation, a situation that has essentially always ex-

---

[5] Rubin G. Cohn, "Public Employee Retirement Plans—the Nature of the Employees' Rights," *Law Forum,* Spring 1968, p. 62.

[6] The significance of investment earnings is discussed more fully in the next chapter.

isted. To improve their odds in the battle against inflation, many public employee retirement systems invest in common stocks, which are widely considered to provide a hedge against inflation. Even if the foregoing were not true, a previous argument might be restated by asking what right the present taxpayer, the one who incurred the $1,000 commitment, has to pass the debt along to the taxpayers 30 years hence.

A response might also be made to the argument about exporting the local government's money. In the first place, it is difficult to maintain a parochial view in the complex financial structure characterizing the present economies of the United States and Canada. Beyond that, any investment out of the local area will return funds in greater amounts as the interest payments or dividend checks are received. In the example cited above the $250 payout resulted in a $1,000 payback, the difference most likely coming from a debtor outside the locality of the government.

Use of the Best Cost Measurement Method. As indicated in Chapter 5, the costs of a retirement system's benefits and of modifying those benefits are best measured by a method currently responsive to the elements making up that cost. This specification for measuring the cost is met only by actuarial cost methods. Such a cost method can be used with any funding method. If the cost and funding methods are the same, however, the system's financing will be better understood. For example, the fiscal implications of a change in the benefits will certainly be more evident, especially to those who are not initiated into the mysteries of pension financing, if the costs are expressed as actual appropriations to be made currently, instead of as theoretical employer commitments.

There is another objection to measuring costs by an actuarial cost method while making employer contributions using the current disbursement method. Inherent in an actuarial cost method is the assumption that normal costs will be less than the benefit payments they are intended to cover, because of interest between the time normal costs are assigned and the time the benefit payments are actually made. The difference between the two cost methods, then, is the hypothetical interest earned in the interim. In the political arena, subtleties such as hypothetical interest are easily lost. Confusion of this sort can be avoided if the employer's contributions follow an actuarial cost method.

A related point of minor importance deals with the expense of determining actuarial costs. As current measures of accruing costs and of costs of benefit changes, nothing takes the place of actuarial costs. They should be calculated regardless of the method the employer is using to finance the retirement system. For example, no legislature would write a blank check in the authorization of a building project—the specific dollar costs would have to be authorized and appropriated. By the same token, no legislature *should* authorize a retirement program without knowing the cost, regardless of how it is to be paid. Thus, the expense of calculating the actuarial cost should be viewed as a necessary adjunct to a retirement system, and not as a deterrent to the use of a funding method.

Flexibility. Funded systems are protected against adverse financial experience by their ability to draw upon their funds when unforeseen needs arise. These needs can occur because of adverse experience, such as an abnormal number of early retirements or an exceptional amount of death or disability benefits resulting from a catastrophe. These needs can also be the result of the employer's facing a fiscal crisis which brings about a temporary stoppage of employer contributions. In either event, the existence of a fund gives the employer flexibility in meeting his commitments under the retirement program. Under a current disbursement method, in contrast, the employer has no flexibility but must meet each payment from current tax revenue. This requirement can be particularly onerous if the adversity coincides with other fiscal problems. This might be the case when, for example, poor economic conditions induce an abnormal number of early retirements or when a catastrophe causes exceptional death or disability payments.

FINANCING FEDERAL OLD-AGE INSURANCE

On occasion the lack of full funding in the two federal old-age programs—U.S. social security and the Canada Pension Plan—has been used as an argument against funding non-federal public employee retirement systems. This argument was omitted from the pros and cons in the previous sections because it is specious, in the author's opinion. For one thing, there is no unanimity of expert opinion that the present way of paying for federal programs is right.[7] Some might contend that using a bad example as a precedent is compounding a felony. Regardless of one's viewpoint on this controversy, there is much less quarrel with the concepts that the federal programs occupy unique positions in the economies of the two nations and that their financial affairs must be handled accordingly.

The following comments were made by a panel of actuaries and economists reporting on their study of the financial policy governing the U.S. social security program:

. . . Relatively large trust funds are [not] necessary for the proper management of the social security system. If it were possible, by accumulating a trust fund invested in obligations of the United States, to lighten the economic burden carried by future generations for the support of the beneficiary part of the population, . . . [higher] tax schedules might be appropriate. But in an economy such as that of the United States, the assumption of a tax burden by a current generation in order to accumulate a trust fund of government obligations will accomplish no such transfer. . . . Excesses of social security contributions over benefits will be used for reducing deficits or increasing surpluses of the unified budget. The securities held by the System and the interest they are projected to earn are simply a claim on future revenues of the government. During any period of time that the trust funds are reduced or interest is used to finance benefits, revenue sources

---

[7] For example, see Ray M. Peterson, "Misconceptions and Missing Perceptions of our Social Security System (Actuarial Anesthesia)," *Transactions, Society of Actuaries,* Vol. 11, p. 812, and the discussion of this paper.

other than the payroll tax will be diverted to finance those benefits.[8]

A basic question here is: Can funding reduce the tax burden in future years? The panel says no. So also, in effect, does Walter Shur in his paper "Financing the Federal Retirement System," published by the Society of Actuaries.[9] Although his attention was primarily focused on the U.S. federal employee systems, the following comments apply equally to social security:

> Those who argue [that funding can reduce future taxes] . . . say that the additional taxes collected to cover the excess of accruing costs over actual benefit disbursements would reduce the need for borrowing from the public. In effect, the government would borrow from the retirement fund [which would become a buyer of government bonds in quantity] instead of from the public . . . Thus, the argument goes, the total Treasury debt and interest on the debt would be unchanged, but a portion of the interest on the debt could be used to pay retirement benefits instead of interest payments to public bondholders.
>
> The proponent of this line of reasoning may think that he is arguing the merits of a reserve plan but, in fact, he is arguing the merits of increased taxation. He is saying that (1) the reserve method will result in higher taxes; (2) higher taxes will result in a transfer of debt from the public to the retirement fund; and (3) the revised fiscal policy implied by (1) and (2) will result in economic growth and stability at least as favorable as without the revision.
>
> If higher taxes will put the economy of the future in a better position to bear the burden of retirement payments, then higher taxes are desirable with or without a reserve method of financing and the point should be argued on economic grounds, not on actuarial grounds.

These arguments against funding the massive federal programs do not transfer to the nonfederal systems. The primary

---

8 *Report of the 1971 Advisory Council on Social Security,* House Document No. 92–80, Washington, 1971.

9 Walter Shur, "Financing the Federal Retirement Systems," *Transactions, Society of Actuaries,* Vol. 16, p. 281. This paper also deals with other aspects of retirement system financing in a lucid manner.

reason for this is that the federal governments are unique in the effect their fiscal and taxing policies have on the economy. Another reason the arguments do not transfer to the local level is the enormity of the portfolio of securities the federal systems would acquire if they were funded. In the United States, for example, if the social security program were being funded, assets of about one-half trillion dollars would have accumulated by 1972. If these assets were represented by U.S. securities, as would be almost certain, the fund would have been greater than all the issues of U.S. bonds and notes actually outstanding at that time. Clearly this puts the financing questions associated with federal old-age programs in a different league from all other retirement systems.

UNFUNDED ACTUARIAL LIABILITY

The *unfunded actuarial liability* is similar in nature to the supplemental cost described in the previous chapter. The primary distinction is that the unfunded actuarial liability gives weight to the value of the actual assets held by the system and is thus a measure of the degree of funding at any time.

At the establishment of a system when no fund exists, the unfunded actuarial liability under any cost method equals the supplemental cost. If subsequent employer contributions are geared to the costs produced by that cost method, the employer payments are the sum of the normal cost, interest on unfunded actuarial liability and an additional amount to liquidate that liability over a period of years. The unfunded actuarial liability at any time is then the initial unfunded actuarial liability reduced by the portion of the annual payments allocated for its amortization. If experience follows the actuarial assumptions, the unfunded actuarial liability will be disposed of over the number of years originally scheduled in the calculation of the total employer contribution rate.

Adopting a program for amortizing the unfunded actuarial liability is a basic step in the financing of a retirement system. Some of the considerations affecting such a decision are similar to those given in Chapter 5 concerning the period to be used for spreading the supplmental cost. An additional point should be noted: The shorter the period chosen, the greater the cushion against adverse future experience. This is particularly important in small systems, where the financial capabilities of the local community may ebb and flow. Establishing a short amortization period builds up the fund and helps it to withstand adverse experience.

A common event disrupting a schedule for amortizing the unfunded actuarial liability is an improvement in the benefit structure. Such an event generally creates an additional unfunded actuarial liability which in turn requires an adjustment in the employer contributions, in the period of amortizing the unfunded actuarial liability or in both. The schedule of liquidating the original unfunded liability may be altered for another reason—the occurrence of actuarial gains and losses.

ACTUARIAL GAINS AND LOSSES

In many public employee retirement systems going the funded route, the employer contributions are set to match costs determined by an actuarial cost method. Because of this, actuarial assumptions come into play. The appropriate costs are calculated on the basis of these assumptions. If the contributions are made precisely to match the costs so generated, the fund grows on schedule to conform with the predictions of the cost method, provided the assumptions are perfect predictors of the future.

Obviously this last proviso is a practical impossibility. The amount computed as the present value of future benefits will not be exactly sufficient to meet all the payments—it may be too much or too little. The employees will not die precisely according to the assumed death rates. The employees will not retire exactly at the assumed time. Interest and dividends will not be earned on the fund exactly as predicted. In these and in other ways, differences will arise between the rates assumed by the actuary and the way things actually happen.

These differences give rise to what are called *actuarial gains and losses.*

The actuarial gain or loss for any period is the difference between the system's actual financial status at the end of the period and its expected status then as estimated by the application of the actuarial assumptions during the period. Thus, for example, the value of the fund at the end of a period can be anticipated by calculating the expected interest earnings on the fund at the beginning and on the money added during the period. If all other actuarial assumptions are precisely realized and the actual fund at the end exceeds the expected fund, a gain from interest earnings has occurred. If the actual fund is deficient, a loss has occurred. If other actuarial assumptions are not precisely realized, a gain or loss from each source is calculated. All of the elements making up the total gain or loss can then be combined to derive the net actuarial gain or loss for the period. In practice, analyzing the gain or loss by source can be quite difficult because of the effects of the various assumptions on each other. For this reason the gain or loss will sometimes be obtained only in total, without an analysis by source. This is done by comparing the total expected actuarial costs with the actual costs as reflected in the changes in the fund balance and value of benefits yet to be paid.

In the typical system, where the employer contribution rate varies from time to time, an actuarial gain results in a tendency for a reduction in the employer contribution rate and an actuarial loss results in a tendency for an increase. Because of this, experience dictates the true costs of the program in the long run; the funding method and actuarial assumptions regulate the varying contribution rates meeting these true costs.

Effect of Actuarial Gains and Losses on Funding.   Each actuarial funding method has its own characteristic way or ways of treating actuarial gains and losses. Under either the projected benefit or the accrued benefit funding method, for example, gains may be used to reduce, and losses to extend, the period of years during which the unfunded actuarial liability is being amortized. If the resulting variation in the period of years is within a range considered acceptable by the system's managers, it is not necessary to change the employer contribution rate whenever an actuarial gain or loss occurs. Thus, barring substantial variations in the actuarial assumptions, employer contribution rates may be relatively stable for several years under such a method, a feature of substantial advantage to a public employee system where contribution rates affect appropriations and budgets are fixed as many as three years in advance.

Another approach to handling actuarial gains and losses can be followed under the projected benefit funding method. Under this approach all gains and losses are spread over the remaining working life of the employees and merged into the current normal costs. Where this approach is used, the normal cost varies from year to year, as the cumulative effects of gains and losses are added or subtracted, but the schedule for amortizing the unfunded actuarial liability is not affected. Actually, because of the dampening effect of spreading them over long periods of time, actuarial gains and losses do not necessarily result in changes in contribution rates of any significant amount from year to year.

A third way of treating actuarial gains and losses is to reflect them immediately in the employer contribution. Under this method the employer contribution is the regular normal cost plus the payment for amortizing the unfunded actuarial liability, plus the total amount of the previous year's actuarial loss, or less the total amount of the previous year's actuarial gain. If the gains or losses are not kept to a minimum, this method can produce rates of employer contribution which vary by substantial amounts.

Failure to Fund. In the normal course of events, an actuarial loss occurs in a funded system if the interest yield is smaller than anticipated, or if pensioners' longevity is greater than expected, or, if for any number of other reasons the employer contributions required by actual experience turn out to be in excess of those made. In like fashion, if the actual employer contributions are below those required by the actuarial cost method being used as a guide, the effect on funding will be the same as if an actuarial loss had occurred. For example, in a time of emergency, all employer contributions may be diverted for other purposes for a year. This will have the effect of extending the period of amortization of the unfunded actuarial liability or of increasing subsequent employer contributions, depending on the way the actuarial gains and losses are being treated.

This aspect of funding adds considerable flexibility to the employer's contribution requirements under a funded system. It also can pose a threat: If the privilege of deferring required contributions is abused, a funded system can become unfunded. If deferral is allowed at all, provident management will set bench marks in its funding program, and will not allow deferral of employer contributions or any of the conventional actuarial losses to drop the funding status below these levels. One commonly used criterion is that the unfunded actuarial liability should not arise above its initial balance,[10] as might otherwise happen if employer contributions were deferred. A second bench mark might be that the relationship between assets and earned benefits for all employees should constantly progress toward parity and reach it within, say, 25 years of the establishment of the system to give an appropriate degree of assurance to the employer's promise to pay benefits. A third control of the misuse of the privilege to defer employer contributions might be the requirement that any such deferrals must be made up with interest within five years.[11] Many other types of guidelines might be used, including combinations of those given above. The basic purpose of any set of such bench marks, of course, is to prevent a system from falling away from its original funding goals. It is

---

10 In private pension plans in the United States, Internal Revenue Service requirements that a plan be permanent have been interpreted to require that this bench mark be met.

11 This type of rule is applied to many Canadian corporations by the federal Pension Benefit Standards Act and by several provincial acts. However it is not applicable to deferrals of employer contributions, but only to any actuarial loss which sets back the required funding of the initial unfunded actuarial liability.

obvious that this purpose can best be carried out if the employer contributions are always made as required by the governing funding method.

Valuation of Assets. As the investments of a system grow, the method used for valuing them plays an increasing role in determining the actuarial gains or losses the system will incur. The portfolios of most systems are made up of securities held for extended periods. This permits the market values of some of the investments to diverge significantly from their costs—the prices paid for them. Valuing a portfolio at cost thus fails to give a realistic value to securities whose market values change substantially, common stocks being the most obvious example. The use of market value gives precision to the current value but creates substantial variability in the asset values. The special asset valuation methods in use are thus designed to strike a balance between two purposes, which are sometimes in opposition:

A recognition of each security's intrinsic value at the time of valuation;

An attempt to gain stability of valuation, so as to avoid fluctuating gains and losses which have no long term significance.

Different asset valuation methods are often employed for the fixed income portfolio (bonds, mortgages, etc.) and the equities (common stocks, convertible bonds, preferred stocks). A fixed income security may be valued at cost or market, or it may be given a value somewhere between its cost and its maturity value. For example, a common method used to value a bond purchased at a discounted price (as compared with the maturity value) is the purchase price increased by the discount accrued ratably to the maturity date. Similarly, if the purchase price of a bond includes a premium above the maturity value, this method puts a value on the bond of the purchase price less an amortization of the premium to the maturity date. Another method values the bond at whatever price is necessary to make the coupons and maturity amount have a yield equal to the interest rate assumed by the actuary in his calculations, regardless of actual cost or market.

In the case of common stocks, various valuation methods in use include cost, market, a weighted average of cost and market, cost improved by an assumed growth rate or by a portion of the retained earnings of the corporations whose stock is held, and variations or combinations of these.

One inherent hazard of special asset valuation methods is the danger that investment decisions might be influenced by the method being used. For example, any method of valuing a security which results in its being valued below the actual market might encourage its sale, even though the security replacing it may have even less potential for yield. In fact, securities with a substantial growth in market value would tend to be sold if such a valuation method were a governing factor while those with little gain would tend to be held. Such a practice could not be considered conducive to good portfolio management.

The influence of valuation methods on investment decisions is overcome in one problem area by the practice known as *bond-swapping*. In a market with rapidly rising interest rates, the price of long-term bonds drops substantially. If a system values each bond at the price paid for it, at its maturity value, or at some amount in between, sale of the bond can substantially reduce the apparent value of the assets held by the system, even if the bond bought to replace the sold security has a greater potential yield. Because of this, many systems are reluctant to sell securities at depressed prices. To give relief in this situation, the "swapping" concept has been widely adopted. Under this method, a replacement bond of about the same quality is bought when the old one is sold. The new bond matures for the same amount and at nearly the same date but usually has a higher coupon rate. The replacement bond is carried on the books of the system at its actual cost plus the loss realized on the sale of the original security. Assume, for example, that an original $1,000 bond was bought for $970 and sold for $900. The bond-swapping method assigns the $70 loss to its replacement. Thus, if the replacement bond was bought for $920, it would be carried at a book value of $990, $920 plus the $70 loss on the original bond's sale. The new discount of $10 ($1,000 par value less $990) is accrued over the lifetime of the replacement bond. This technique eliminates an artificial dip in the asset value which would otherwise create an actuarial loss.

Actuarial Revaluation Gains and Losses. All of the actuarial gains and losses discussed so far are called *actuarial experience gains and losses.* A second category of gain and loss is called *actuarial revaluation gains and losses.* These arise when the actuarial assumptions are changed to reflect a reassessment of anticipated experience.

As an example, a system's future employer commitments may have been calculated on the assumption that the portfolio of investments held by the system, and those to be purchased in the future, will earn 4 percent compound interest per year. Because of a change in the investment market or in the system's investment philosophy, the actuary of the system may feel a 5 percent interest assumption is justified for future yields. Accordingly, all of the future payments to members and their beneficiaries would be revalued at the higher rate. This reduces the present value of these commitments, since a greater portion of the disbursements are assumed to come from interest earnings. The normal costs and unfunded actuarial liabilities would also be recalculated and the results would be lower for the same reason.

The gain that results from this procedure is an actuarial revaluation gain. If the new assumptions result in increased liabilities, an actuarial revaluation loss would result. In either case, the gain or loss could be treated as are all other actuarial gains or losses for the system. Alternatively, because of the special nature of the gain or loss, special treatment could be given appropriate to the new funding status of the system.

EMPLOYER CONTRIBUTION RATES

When the actuarial cost method has been determined, the actuarial assumptions set, and the data gathered for valuation, all of the raw materials are at hand for budgeting the current employer cost or, if the employer contribution rate is fixed by statute, testing the rate's adequacy. Although the specific technique varies, depending upon the size of the system and other characteristics peculiar to the group of employees in the valuation, the process is essentially one of adding together costs associated with each employee. The costs for each employee are produced by evaluating each of the potential benefit payments for which the employee or his beneficiary might become eligible and determining the probability of the payment occurring. If a projection is being made for the purpose of estimating costs on a pay-as-you-go method, each payment is associated with all others expected to occur in a particular year, to obtain the total estimate of payments in that year. If a valuation is being made for the purpose of funding benefits in advance, each of these future payments is discounted at the assumed interest rate to the date of valuation.

In some instances, the results of the valuation are expressed in terms of a projected employer contribution rate as a percentage of salary. If the actuarial assumptions are realized in the developing experience, the regular contribution into the system's fund of an amount of money equal to the determined percentage of payroll of the covered employees sets aside sufficient funds to meet the commitments of the system, all in accordance with the actuarial cost method used. The required contribution is often expressed as a range of rates within which satisfactory funding will occur. The difference between the contribution at the low and at the high rate is generally the difference between amortizing the unfunded actuarial liability over the longest acceptable time versus the shortest such period.

The governing boards of many systems have the right and responsibility to set the employer contribution rates. After receiving the actuarial report giving the range of acceptable contribution rates, each board acts to specify the rate to be used in determining the employer contributions. The choice of rate within the acceptable range is often governed by decisions to amortize the unfunded liability in a specified period and to maintain a reasonably stable rate. The rate chosen remains in force until a subsequent valuation is performed. A modification of the rate takes place then if the new valuation so indicates. This general approach is probably the best from an actuarial viewpoint, particularly if the board is required to take corrective action if the employer contribution rates fall outside the specified range. If the discretionary power of the board is too wide, it might take on a legislative function since its actions could affect the budgetary authority of the legislative body.

In some systems, the legislative body retains its full budgetary discretion through specifying by law what the employer contribution rate is to be. If this is regularly modified pursuant to actuarial review, the effect is much the same as if this responsibility is passed along to a retirement board. The potential pitfall of this method is that a budgetary imbalance can be eased by failing to make such increases in the employer contribution rates as are called for by an actuarial valuation. The temptation can be strong since failure to take action rarely results in any immediate shortage of cash in the funds of the retirement system.

Where the employer contribution rate is specified as a percentage of salary, the necessary contribution can be treated as a payroll expense and need not be budgeted independently from other salary-related expenditures. In some systems, the specific dollar amount required to meet the entire employer contribution from legislative session to legislative session is treated as a separate item under the budget. This method probably faces the greatest peril of legislative irresponsibility in retirement system financing of any method except the pay-as-you-go method.

In many smaller systems the employer contribution matches the employee contribution on a dollar-for-dollar basis. If an employee terminates before his benefit is vested, the employer contributions matching the refunded employee contributions are released often to help meet the required employer's contribution for other employees. One variation of this approach allows the employer to anticipate future employee terminations and thereby only partially match employee contributions on a current basis. When an employee retires, the difference needed is made up from unallocated employer funds. A second variation is to make similar contributions but not allocate any of the employer money to any particular employee until he retires. At that point, the pool of unallocated money is drawn upon to provide a sum equal to the employee's accumulated contributions.

Chapter 7

Investments

MAJOR DIFFERENCES between private plans and public employee retirement systems are found in the theories and practices of investing accumulated money. One of these differences is derived from legal strictures upon the investment authority of the public systems. A second difference is the tendency of some public systems, especially in Canada, to hold substantial portions of their funds in public securities, primarily in the municipal bond market.

In a mature retirement system operating on a funded basis, the annual income from interest and dividends may equal or exceed the amount being contributed to the fund by the employer. If the two sources of income should be equal, an increase in the yield rate on the fund from 4 percent to 5 percent, as an example, will increase investment income by 25 percent and decrease the tax burden of the system by 25 percent. Rarely does a shift that dramatic occur swiftly enough to be widely noticed. Nevertheless, the importance of investment return must be emphasized: Every additional dollar received in interest and dividends means a dollar saved, either in taxes if the gain is in the employer portion of the fund, or in the employee's pocket if the extra earnings are on his part of the fund.

This chapter examines the topic of investments in public employee retirement systems. The legal limitations placed upon investing authority will be reviewed, as will the general elements of investment strategy within those limitations.

THE SIGNIFICANCE OF INVESTMENT YIELD

In the previous chapter, the funding of a retirement system's liabilities was discussed. Briefly, in a funded plan the contributions for any employee will be completed during the working lifetime of that employee, creating a fund at retirement from which the retirement benefits will be drawn. Since the contributions will be unused for some period of time, they can be invested. The importance of the role of investments may be more easily grasped by considering the following oversimplified example. Suppose a woman retires at age 60 and lives exactly 20 years thereafter, which is approximately her life expectancy. If she had entered employment at age 40, one might visualize each year's payment of her retirement income as coming from a contribution 20 years earlier. The contribution made while she was 40 could be thought of as paying the benefit when she is 60, that made while she was 41 as paying the benefit when she is 61, and so forth. If there were no interest available on the money deposited for her, the same amount would have to be contributed as is ultimately withdrawn. Thus, if her benefit is $3,000 a year, $3,000 must be deposited each year. Actually, of course, the money will be invested and earn interest.

If the rate of interest on the investment should average 3.5 percent, a relatively low level at present-day standards, the money will double during the 20 year period. Where a $3,000 annual contribution would be necessary to pay her benefits if no interest were earned, only $1,500 would be required if the money were invested at 3.5 percent.

Higher rates of interest will reduce the required contributions still more, as illustrated in the following table:

Rate of Annual Interest (%)	Approximate Annual Contribution	Ratio of This Contribution to That at 0%
0	$3,000	100%
3.5	1,500	50
5.5	1,000	33
7	750	25
9.5	500	17

Almost as remarkable as the differences between the numbers in this table is the fact that interest rates covering nearly the entire range of the table have been experienced over the 25 year period ended in 1970. At the low end, the average yields on high-grade municipal bonds in 1946 were only slightly over 1.5 percent, the corresponding figure for U.S. government bonds being 2.19 percent.[1] At the other extreme, yields of 9 percent or greater were obtainable on occasion for top-grade securities in the latter part of the period, when even some short-term U.S. government bonds yielded in excess of 8 percent.

Still greater yields were available for the investor willing to take the risk of periodic declines in values and yields. A study encompassing every stock listed on the New York Stock Exchange, for example, showed that for the longest period studied (1926–1960), an average annual rate of yield of 9 percent was experienced. For a 10 year period commencing in December, 1950, a rate of yield of nearly 15 percent was experienced. This study hypothesized the investment of equal amounts of money in each company having shares listed on the New York Stock Exchange and reinvesting dividends.[2]

To some extent, of course, the differences in yield are the result of changes in economic conditions and are completely

---

[1] U.S. Bureau of the Census, *Historical Statistics of the United States, Colonial Times to 1957* (Washington, 1960), Tables X330 and X331.

[2] Lawrence Fisher and James H. Lorie, "Rates of Return on Investments and Common Stocks," *Journal of Business* (Graduate School of Business, University of Chicago, January 1964).

outside the power of any investor to control. As an indication of the variability at the conservative end of the spectrum, the average yields on long-term U.S. government bonds in a 50 year period dropped from over 5 percent in the early 1920s to a low of 2.05 percent in 1941 and then climbed again to a high of 6.59 percent in 1970.[3] In the example given earlier, the required contribution for a $3,000 per year pension would vary from $918 to $1,999 dollars at the extreme years of 1941 and 1970, assuming that the system was fully invested in U.S. government bonds and that the bonds maintained a constant yield at precisely the specified level for 40 years.

TYPES OF INVESTMENT AND YIELDS

Although no system has the power to alter the bond-yield cycle, most systems can pick from a wide array of securities in investing their available funds at any point in time. The importance of the choice has caused greater attention to be devoted recently to this aspect of fund management. The trend has been toward more aggressive investment policies and liberalization of statutes governing the investment powers of public employee retirement systems. These moves to more progressive investment policies have come during a period of booming growth in the assets of the plan, making the shift in investment philosophy all the more significant.

Investments of U.S. Systems. Table 4 summarizes the overall shift in the investments of U.S. systems during the 1960s. Although the assets of the state and local systems nearly tripled during the decade, the holdings of federal bonds decreased by more than 10 percent, causing their share of the total investment to drop from about 1/3 to about 1/10. Even more spectacular was the reduction in the dollar amount of state and local bonds, bringing them from approximately 23 percent of the total investment to about 4

[3] *Federal Reserve Bulletins;* Bureau of Census, *Historical Statistics:* Series X330. This series is made up of unweighted averages of the yields of all outstanding U.S. bonds due or callable after a minimum period, that minimum period being 8, 10, 12, or 15 years at various times.

TABLE 4
Assets of State and Local Retirement Systems in the United States (in billions)

	1960	1970		
	All Systems	*All Systems*	*State-Ad-ministered*	*Locally-Ad-ministered*
Federal Bonds	$ 6.0	$ 5.2	$ 3.2	$ 1.9
State and Local Bonds	4.3	2.2	.6	1.6
Total Government Bonds	$10.3	$ 7.3	$ 3.8	$ 3.5
Corporate Bonds	6.0	30.1	22.7	7.5
Mortgages	1.2	6.6	5.8	.8
Corporate Stocks	.4	6.9	5.1	1.8
Other	.6	4.0	2.5	1.4
Total	$18.5	$54.9	$40.0	$15.0

Note: Because of rounding, detail may not add to totals.
Source: U.S. Bureau of Census reports (GF Series, No. 2). Bond figures are par values; all others are book values. Data are derived from surveys of individual systems. Each system's data are as of its fiscal year ended in first half of given year or last half of previous year.

percent. The slack was taken up fairly evenly by all other types of investments, corporate bonds increasing from ⅓ to better than ½ of the total investment, and mortgages nearly doubling their share of the investment portfolios to more than 10 percent of the total. The greatest percentage increase was registered by corporate stocks, whose share increased from 2 percent to 12 percent.

In all cases the shift was from the conservative to the more venturesome investment, offering the prospect of higher yield. What has caused this shift? Among the reasons are the following:

Competition. This has occurred both between the various public employee systems, and between public and private plans. As public systems have grown, their staffs have increasingly shared their experiences and compared results. The phenomenal growth in private retirement plans during the 1950s and 1960s also resulted in aggressive investment policies which were widely reported and analyzed.

Growth in common stock values. The prosperity of most of the 1950s and 1960s brought outstanding growth to the values of common stocks, making them more attractive as their effective yields outstripped those of fixed income investments.

Inflation. The continuing deterioration in the value of the dollar made increases in benefits necessary; improved investment yields were one method of meeting the additional costs. This factor was in greater evidence as benefits were increased for retired members whose pensions had not keep pace with the cost of living.

Increasing taxes. The ever-present and increasing demands on the taxpayer, particularly at the state and local level, directed attention to more sophisticated means of reducing tax commitments. Of these, a painless one was to cause the investments of the retirement systems to go farther, through a shift to securities with more attractive yields.

As Table 4 shows, locally administered systems held a much higher share of their 1970 investments in government bonds than did state-administered systems. The distinction was most apparent in the investments in state and local bonds. State-administered plans held less than 2 percent of their portfolio in such bonds, while the local plans held 11 percent in this manner. To a large extent, this disparity is attributable to the tendency of the local funds to invest in local issues.

There are significant disadvantages in the practice of public employee retirement systems investing in municipal bonds, particularly those bonds issued locally. One objection is that the yield on municipal bonds in the United States is artificially depressed, due to their tax-free status in the hands of private investors. This tax advantage is of no value to a retirement system, since it pays no taxes. Moreover, where there is some community of decision between the investing authority (the local retirement fund) and the political subdivision issuing the bonds, unwise investments can easily occur. This is particularly true in the case of revenue bonds, which might not be supportable on the open market but which are purchased by the local retirement fund, in effect subsidizing the borrowing authority. Another objection to investment by a local fund in its own securities is the lack of diversification. If the political entity should come upon hard times, its failure to meet its commitments would be doubly burdensome if the investments of its retirement fund were in its own securities.

The investment techniques of systems administered at the state and local levels also differed in the wider use of mortgages by the state-administered systems. Nearly 15 percent of state-administered funds versus 5 percent of locally administered funds were invested in mortgages in 1970. Legal restrictions on investments of the local funds may contribute to this difference. Another reason for the difference is the difficulty retirement systems, especially small ones, have in administering mortgages. A common practice of the larger retirement funds is to buy substantial blocks of mortgages ($500 thousand, $1 million, etc.) which are administered by mortgage bankers. The retirement fund becomes involved in the actual details of any one mortgage only in exceptional circumstances. Small retirement systems do not have sufficient funds to move easily into this type of market.

Because of the differences described above, it would seem reasonable for locally administered systems to have lower investment yields than state systems. There is some evidence to support this thesis, but it is meager and of marginal statistical significance. Obtaining comparative yields with precision is made difficult by wide variations in accounting methods. Based upon a study of all public employee systems in the United States, an average yield relative to the book value of all assets was found to be about 4.47 percent for state-administered plans and 4.35 percent for locally administered plans. These figures were derived from a Bureau of Census study[4] of the fiscal years ending in the latter half of 1967 and the first half of 1968. The figures are probably understated to the extent that capital gains from the increase in value of common stocks were not included. Had capital gains been

---

[4] U.S. Bureau of the Census, *1967 Census of Governments*, Vol. 6, Topical Studies No. 2.

included, the relative standing of the state-administered funds would probably have improved, albeit very slightly.

Investments of Canadian Systems. The distribution of assets in Canadian public employee retirement systems is significantly different from that found in the United States. Table 5 presents Canadian data corresponding approximately to the U.S. data in Table 4. Provincial and local bonds make up over 70 percent of the assets of Canadian systems, as compared with about 4 percent in the corresponding systems in the United States. In all of the other categories of investment shown in the table, including federal bonds, the Canadian percentages are smaller than the corresponding U.S. percentages. The statistics presented in Table 5 were derived from an analysis which includes a further breakdown among municipalities, provincial governments, and educational institutions. These statistics show remarkable homogeneity as to investment percentages in the various categories listed. The only significant exception to this is in government bonds where, not surprisingly, the municipalities are heavily invested in municipal bonds.

Despite the preponderance of government bonds in Canadian portfolios, the average yields were substantially above the U.S. average. For comparable fiscal years in 1968, the

TABLE 5
Assets of Provincial and Local Retirement Systems in Canada (in millions)

	1960	1970
Federal Bonds	$ 77	$ 109
Provincial and Local Bonds	629	2,161
Total Government Bonds	$706	$2,270
Corporate Bonds	31	175
Mortgages	6	83
Corporate Stocks	7	151
Other	49	250
Total	$799	$2,929

Source: Statistics Canada Reports (74–201). All figures are book values. Data are derived from surveys of individual systems. Each system's data are as of its fiscal year ended in first half of given year or last half of previous year.

approximate Canadian yield was 5.45 percent; the U.S. figure was 4.43 percent. In analyzing this differential one should keep the following points in mind:

1. Yields on Canadian securities in general are significantly higher than those on U.S. securities. For example, in 1968, the average yields on Canadian federal government bonds (of ten year maturity or greater) was 6.75 percent, while the corresponding U.S. figure was 5.5 percent.

2. Yields on Canadian provincial and local bonds, in particular, are substantially higher than those of corresponding securities in the United States. Not only is there greater competition for capital funds in Canada, leading to higher yield rates on all types of investments, but interest on Canadian municipal bonds is fully taxable. On the other hand, interest on U.S. municipal bonds is tax-free in the hands of many investors, improving the marketability of the bonds but reducing their yield. Continuing the previous example, 10 provincial bonds had an average yield of 7.60 percent in 1968 while bonds of 10 Canadian municipalities were yielding 7.80 percent.[5] In contrast 15 U.S. municipal bonds had an average yield in 1968 of 4.51 percent.[6]

Comparative Yields of Insurance Companies.   Lest one with responsibilities for Canadian retirement system funds be overly smug about the comparison of Canadian and U.S. rates, it would be in order to present a brief comparison of investment yields of life insurance companies, which are in similar positions of trust for the protection of the principal of funds given them and which often have similar investment restrictions placed on them by law. In 1968, federally registered Canadian insurance companies showed an average yield of 6.03 percent on their investments, more than one half of 1 percent better than the yields of public employee retirement systems. For comparison the average yields of U.S. insurance companies were 4.95 percent in 1968, likewise being more than one half of 1 percent greater than the average yields of

---

5 Bank of Canada Statistical Summary, November 1971.

6 Standard and Poor's Index, *Statistical Abstract of the United States*, 1969, Table 665.

the public employee retirement systems. Some of this difference may be due to the competitive nature of the life insurance business. Some may be due to differences in the laws governing the two types of investments. Whatever the reason, if the differential of one half of 1 percent could have been transformed into additional income to the public employee retirement systems, the taxpayers of the United States and Canada would have saved approximately a quarter of a billion dollars in 1968.

INVESTMENT STRATEGY AND
LEGAL RESTRICTIONS

The decision of how much to invest in various categories of available securities can often be reduced to a weighing of the elements of prospective yield and risk. Since the market for capital funds tends to require higher yields for riskier investments, the receipt of greater yield generally involves forfeiture of some of the security of investment. The balancing of these factors is highly subjective and there appears to be no firm and final resolution of the problem of finding the ideal investment strategy for a pension fund.

A complicating question, however, involves the restrictions placed upon investments of public employee retirement funds. While some legislative authorities regularly review the question of investments, the subject in other locales seems to have suffered from neglect. Overly conservative investment practices often exemplify this neglect. An indication of such conservatism, for example, might be holding more than half of the investment portfolio in cash deposits and government securities. This criterion was met in 26 states by either state-administered funds or locally administered funds or both in 1968. Obviously, arguments can be advanced for such investment policy, at least with respect to investment in government securities, but the effect of such a policy upon yield is substantial. The aggregate yield of the systems involved was 4.06 percent in 1968, compared with 4.43 percent in all systems in the United States.

Examples of Investment Policy. Some specific examples illustrate the effect of investment policy upon yield. In one state, the two major systems, with total assets of nearly two thirds of a billion dollars at June 30, 1968, held approximately 60 percent of these assets in federal bonds. The yields of these two systems were 3.91 percent and 4.17 percent respectively, calculated on the same basis as the 4.43 percent yield for all U.S. systems. Another state where over 80 percent of nearly $200 million in assets was invested in federal bonds, experienced a yield of only 3.67 percent. The system of a large county in the same state had all its investments in government bonds or deposits and showed a yield of 3.75 percent.

An example of what a change in investment policy can do is offered by the Teachers' Retirement System of Louisiana. On June 30, 1968, more than three quarters of its assets were in municipal and U.S. treasury bonds. The yield for the previous year, calculated on the same basis as the yields quoted in the last few paragraphs, was 3.79 percent. As a result of a large disinvestment of government bonds and heavy investment of the proceeds plus new cash in corporate bonds and stocks, the yield for the year ended June 30, 1969 increased to over 5 percent. The investment earnings for the year were more than $7 million greater than in the previous year, equivalent to approximately 25 percent of the state's contributions.

Legal Restrictions. The investment policies of public employee retirement systems result from the interaction of the investing authority and the legal restrictions on investments imposed by the legislature. Statutory restrictions generally have the purpose of protecting the principal of the money contributed by the employees and by the government. The laws act as a brake on any tendency to overreact to the pressure for increased yields. One argument holds that the attractive yields resulting from the more aggressive investment techniques have been compiled during a period of prosperity; statutory restrictions protect against the losses of capital which accompany poor times.

A further legal consideration exists when common stocks are owned. Instead of being in the position of a lienholder, as is inherent with the ownership of bonds and mortgages, an investor in common stocks owns a portion of the business. This runs counter to constitutional prohibitions in some states, on the theory that the state is lending its financial support to a corporation by buying its stock. Where such restrictions are contained in a constitution, they can be very cumbersome to remove. Nevertheless, popular votes to eliminate constitutional restrictions have been successful in some jurisdictions.[7]

Public employee retirement systems rarely have investment authority as broad as that of private plans. Generally the laws either specifically prescribe the areas in which investments can be made or indicate that the investment policy is governed by the same laws that apply to life insurance companies.

Solvency. Although there are similarities in the investment goals of pension plans and life insurance companies, there are also differences which argue for fewer restrictions on retirement funds. A discussion of the investment goals of life insurance companies in McGill's *Life Insurance* points out that, "The primary concern of life companies is the risk of legal insolvency, that is, a condition in which admitted assets are less than the liabilities required by law."[8] In turn, this problem is related to the very limited amount of capital and surplus which life insurance companies have as a percentage of their total assets (8.4 percent in 1970). McGill went on to say:

> With company surplus limited to such relatively small proportions, it follows that there is little margin for wide independent fluctuations in the values of either assets or liabilities. But, since liabilities are relatively stable and predictable, the primary insolvency risk centers on the potential loss of value of assets.[9]

---

[7] The states of California and Washington are examples.

[8] Dan M. McGill, *Life Insurance*, rev. ed. (Homewood, Ill.: Richard D. Irwin, Inc., 1967), p. 843.

[9] Ibid.

It is little wonder that life insurance companies and the laws governing them place such a premium on safety of principal.[10] On the other hand, as long as the employer is ultimately responsible for paying benefits and is adequately capitalized, there is no real risk of "legal insolvency" under a pension plan. A pension plan can take greater investment risk than an insurance company without fear of depleting "surplus," since surplus can, in effect, be replenished by the employer over a period of time.

In a somewhat different sense, the hazard for a life insurance company is also technical in nature: It must retain its legal solvency at all points in time, and it cannot rely upon recovery from a temporary slump in asset values or from an adverse swing in mortality experience to bring it out of the hole. The status of a pension plan at any one point in time is far less vital, as pointed out by Frank M. Redington in his address as president of the British Institute of Actuaries:

> Pension schemes can . . . be . . . regarded as homing on to a distant and moving target under the guidance of the actuarial radar tracking system. Whether a scheme will be successful or not is only in part a question of where it is now; that is to say, its current degree of solvency. It is also largely a question of the power of its driving force to bring it curving on to track in due course. The main driving force is the ability of the employer to fulfill his obligations and to increase his contributions whenever necessary. Solvency is, therefore, often inextricably bound up with the resources of the employer.[11]

POLITICAL CONSIDERATIONS

Wherever the balance is struck on legislative control, there is an additional indirect pressure for conservatism in investment, beyond the legal restrictions, because of the public

---

[10] Life insurance companies can be more venturesome in the investment of assets allocated to pension reserves, particularly if guarantees of principal are not made. If a segregated fund is used, the total investment risk is usually with the employer, rather than with the life insurance company.

[11] *Journal of the Institute of Actuaries* (London, 1959) , Vol. 135, p. 6.

nature of the retirement systems. While the investing officer of a corporate retirement fund need only justify his decisions to the management or the directors of the corporation, the investor for a public fund not only must satisfy similar interests but also must be prepared to make a defense before the general public, often in the glare of an adverse press. This hazard is aggravated by the ordinary person's lack of sophistication in investment matters and by the ever-present opportunist ready to make political hay of some event involving public figures.

Another politically sensitive aspect of investments involves the pressures for local investment, either in the bonds of the local government or in private investments, such as corporate bonds or mortgages. Arguments against investment in municipal bonds were given earlier in this chapter. Where private investments are involved, retirement systems often invest their funds to benefit the local economy.

For example, some systems invest locally if a yield can be obtained within a certain percentage of that available for comparable nonlocal investments. The resulting loss of income to the system has to be replaced by taxes. The net effect, then, of such a policy is really a subsidy of local borrowers by the taxpayers, although this is rarely recognized explicitly as such. As the funds held by many public employee retirement systems get larger, a small interest differential can grow to be a substantial subsidy. Even if local investments are favored only when the yields are otherwise equal to those obtainable on comparable investments elsewhere, equality is often a matter of judgment easily affected by extraneous considerations where local investments are concerned. Criteria limited to financial considerations minimize the risk of ill-judged local investments.

Proposals have been made on occasion to use the funds of public employee retirement systems to subsidize ecological investments. This question is similar to that involving local investment of retirement funds. If the investments are at competitive yields and risks, they can be purchased without special consideration. However, if retirement funds take lower yields for this type of investment, the true cost of the ecological investment is masked, as is the true cost of the retirement program.

Political considerations become a factor for other reasons when public employee retirement systems own common stocks. Since stock ownership carries with it the right to vote at stockholder meetings, the retirement system may be called upon to take positions on controversial corporate issues. One theory rather widely accepted in this area is that ownership of stock is inherently a subscription to the practices of management: If management is inferior, the stock should be sold. Therefore, by this theory, the votes of the retirement system stock should be in support of management's position on controversial issues. It should be noted, however, that some retirement systems use their votes to try to influence corporate management on issues that are believed to affect the systems or the political bodies which contribute to the systems.

PROFESSIONAL INVESTMENT MANAGEMENT

Various methods are used to insulate the investing authority from political pressures and to provide professional investment guidance. Having trained investment managers on the system's staff is a step in this direction. A major share of the responsibility for the investment strategy can then be transferred from the politically sensitive retirement system boards to the investment managers and their staffs.

The research and expense advantages of larger staffs can be obtained by the use of unified investment authorities. These exist in various forms in Minnesota, New Jersey, New Mexico, Oregon, and Wisconsin. The Wisconsin Investment Board is a good example. It exercises exclusive control of the investments of the major pension funds in the state of Wisconsin. Seven trustees, who are appointed by the governor and confirmed by the senate, direct a staff of professional investment men. On June 30, 1971, the funds managed by the Board totaled about $1.7 billion, including over $600 million in common stocks.

The Wisconsin Investment Board also uses outside investment counsel to augment the Board's research capabilities in the areas of common and preferred stocks. Retirement systems in many other states also obtain investment counsel, either to make final investment decisions or, more commonly, to provide advice to the systems' staffs. The advice of the investment counsel is often required, sometimes by law, with respect to common stock investments.

Purchasing mutual funds is another way to transfer investment authority to an entity outside the system's control. Once the system makes its choice of funds, it is relieved of further decisions; the control of the regular buying and selling of securities then rests with the management of the mutual funds.

Of a similar nature is the commitment of funds to an insurance company, trust company, or bank trust department for investment. Such investment institutions have many of the features of mutual funds, since the money can be pooled with the funds of other retirement plans. The investment decisions are then made solely by the bank, trust company or insurance company. These organizations also make investment staff available to large retirement systems as investment counsel, either with complete responsibility for the investments or as advisors to the investing authority of the retirement system as to the securities to be purchased and sold.

Most large public employee retirement systems have not delegated broad investment discretion to funding institutions of the sort described in the previous paragraph. In fact, legislatures have generally not granted the right of such delegation to any retirement system. An exception is the Idaho Public Employee Retirement System, where investments are held in trust by two banks, one local and one in New York. The bank trust departments make investments under the broad guidelines imposed upon them by the retirement board of the system. In 1969, incidentally, the Idaho system had the largest percentage (47 percent) of stock investments of any of the large systems of the United States and Canada.[12]

The importance of professional guidance in the investment area is being increasingly recognized. In fact, some large public employee retirement systems are following the lead of large private pension plans in using multiple investment managers, particularly for their common stock portfolios. An example is the New York City Teachers Retirement System, which uses ten separate investment managers for its variable annuity program—one insurance company, five bank and trust companies, two broker-dealers, and two investment management companies.

Public employee retirement systems are turning to investments of a more sophisticated nature as they shift their funds from governmental securities into mortgages, corporate bonds, stocks, and even such exotic forms of investment as real estate, private placements, and purchase-leasebacks. The funds being shifted and the new money to be invested are staggering. The pattern of growth indicated for public employee retirement system funds in the past few years, as exemplified in Tables 4 and 5, is expected to continue to make available unprecedented sums for investment. Projections indicate new capital funds generated by these systems will exceed ten billion dollars per year in the 1980s.[13]

---

[12] Investment Bankers Association of America, *State and Local Pension Funds 1970* (Washington, D.C., 1970).

[13] Daniel M. Holland, *Private Pension Funds: Projected Growth* (New York: National Bureau of Economic Research, 1966).

Chapter 8

Administration

THE ADMINISTRATIVE structure of a public employee retirement system is usually headed by a retirement board or a chief officer, whose primary function is the overall direction of the system within the bounds prescribed by the system's controlling statute. In a large system the board employs an executive director, who in turn hires necessary staff assistance. In addition to full-time staff, which may include persons having specialized technical skills, some part-time help of a professional nature is generally needed. The functions carried out by this administrative organization are described in this chapter.

RETIREMENT BOARD

Nearly all public employee retirement systems place the ultimate responsibility for administration in a governing board. The duties of the board range from making fundamental policy decisions to handling minute administrative details. Policy-making responsibilities include selection of top staff personnel, setting of basic investment goals, review and approval of budgets for administrative expenses and payroll,

and establishment of regulations governing benefit determinations within the broad scope of the law. The extent to
which the board moves beyond policy-making decisions into
the execution and administration of this policy depends upon
the size of the system and its supporting staff, and the traditional and political environment within which the system
operates. The board of a small system without a paid staff
carries out its own decisions. The board of a larger system,
while divesting itself of many details, may retain direct
responsibility in the more sensitive areas which might otherwise be passed along to staff. Examples of the responsibilities
often retained are the authorization of specific investments,
and review and approval of disability claims. These are areas
having substantial importance for financial or political reasons, or because of their effect on public or personnel relations.

A board's sensitivity to influences of the sort just mentioned is affected by the method used to choose its members.
The employees covered by the system are often represented
by one or more board members. Such a member may be
appointed by the governor or by some other elected official,
or he may be elected by the employees themselves. Other
members of the board generally represent the employer or
employers. Employer representation is commonly ex officio:
the attorney general, the superintendent of schools, the city
clerk, and so forth. In some systems representatives of the
general public are also included on the board.

Automatic appointment of officials to retirement boards
has occasionally drawn criticism.[1] The objection raised is
that the ex officio member of the board does not necessarily
have the background, qualifications, or, for that matter,
interest, to serve well on the board. The validity of this
objection must be assessed in each individual case.

In a few large systems, the most notable example being the

---

[1] For example: "Ex officio representation of elected officials is not recommended for a retirement board. It has numerous weaknesses and generally
few advantages." *Accounting and Operating Handbook for Public Employee
Retirement Systems* (Chicago, Ill.: Municipal Finance Officers Association,
1966) .

New York State Employees' Retirement System, a single person has the responsibility normally vested with a board. In New York that person is the state comptroller. Similar officials have corresponding functions in Delaware and Florida.

Some observers believe that the next several years will bring a change in the composition of a number of retirement boards, especially those of the larger systems in the United States. This change is expected to follow the pattern which has emerged in the area of negotiated pension plans in the private sector, to a large extent because of federal legislation. As collective bargaining in public employment becomes more prevalent, it is expected there will evolve a more formal recognition of employer and employee members of the board as such. They will tend to be distributed equally on each board and expected to act, at least to some extent, as spokesmen for their respective interests. If this change occurs generally, it will bring mixed blessings. It may help to assure employees of adequate attention to their interests at an administrative level. It may also help to define more clearly any issues separating the two parties and perhaps lead more easily to solutions. On the other hand, factional division of a board is likely to slow down its deliberations and lead to separate viewpoints on many questions, regardless of the importance of the question to the respective parties. Board members may place their responsibilities to their interests above their responsibilities to the well-being of the system itself.

ADMINISTRATIVE STAFF

A major responsibility of the board is the appointment of the director or executive secretary of the system. In theory, the responsibilities and courses of action of the person so appointed flow from the board. In practice, the director (by whatever title he goes) not only carries out the precepts handed down by the board, including being its emissary to the legislative body and to the employee groups, but also provides substantial guidance to the board. The board often looks to its director for reactions to legislative proposals, for suggested changes in investment policy, and for guidance through the tortuous ravelments involved in the financing of the system. The director may be acquainted with the national trends in public retirement programs through his attendance at meetings discussing these trends. He generally receives the reports made by the technical advisors (such as the actuary, investment counsel, auditor, lawyer, and medical director). Since he usually is the board's spokesman to the legislature, he is also the target upon whom the lobbyists converge when changes in the law are contemplated. Often his most important attribute will be the ability to apprise his board of trends, both local, as expressed to him by the various interest groups, and national, where activities in a few systems may be the bellwether of future local changes. If he is unable to convince his board of the advisability of a particular course of action he prefers (for example, on legislation for benefit improvements), he must be able to represent his board's stand in discussions with other parties, despite his personal preferences.

The director of a small system may serve only part-time, acting as director because of responsibilities in another area (such as city clerk or personnel director). The director of a large system will have a staff and be responsible for its selection. He will often delegate a large portion of his day-to-day administrative responsibilities to an assistant in order to better carry out the functions described in the previous paragraph.

TECHNICAL STAFF

A retirement system needs technical expertise of a specialized nature. Of the various specialties, the actuarial is probably the least understood, because of its relatively infrequent application in other fields.

Actuarial. If the example used in the introduction to Chapter 6 may be called upon again, the actuary is the hydraulics engineer who compares the flow of funds into the fiscal reservoir with the anticipated outflow to pensioners. The skill which sets him apart from the accountant, for example, is the application of probabilities involving life contingencies to the financing of the system. The actuary's tools must be sufficient to handle the complicated benefit structure and financing arrangements which typify retirement systems today. He must also be able to express the results of his estimates of financing needs in a manner that can be understood by the system's staff and board. It is doubly important that the actuary be understood because he needs feedback from the staff, both in checking the appropriateness of the assumptions he regularly uses as to future experience and in making estimates of the effect on these assumptions of potential changes in benefits or employment characteristics. Another duty the actuary is often called upon to perform is the calculation or verification of the amount of benefits payable to individual retirees. Finally, because a great portion of the actuary's experience is in the field of retirement programs, he often advises in the general areas of benefit design, planning and administrative procedures, in addition to the technical areas which are his specialty.

Accounting. Retirement systems also require technical help in the field of accounting. The accountant provides the board and other staff members, including the actuary, with financial statistics regarding the fund's investments. The accountant is generally responsible for establishing and updating the method of maintaining records of each participant's contributions and of those of the employer on his behalf. A computerized processing system is often used for this purpose in large systems. Such a system requires proper accounting controls to minimize errors, particularly where a number of agencies and political subdivisions participate. The processing system usually handles the collection of member and employer contributions from the various agencies, which sometimes number in the hundreds. An efficient method of processing accounts receivable improves the interest earnings of the retirement system by facilitating prompt collections.

The accountant for a public employee retirement system often must work within the framework of accounting practices established for other state, provincial, or municipal purposes. Improvements in accounting practices can be impeded or prohibited by legislative restraints. While these restraints have the basic purpose of protecting the taxpayer from misuse of public funds, they may also impose severe obstacles in the way of efficient practice, particularly because of the distinctive characteristics of retirement systems.

A problem faced by accountants for all pension plans, public and private, is that the largest liability on the balance sheet is the value of future pensions to participants and their beneficiaries. This liability cannot be inventoried without actuarial assistance and is subject to gains and losses which do not fit into conventional bookkeeping niches. Of a similar nature is the basic problem of determining the current costs associated with the financing of a pension plan. This has been the source of controversy for many years, but a 1966 opinion of the Accounting Principles Board of the American Institute of Certified Public Accountants produced a standard against which accounting methods can now be compared.[2]

Legal. Competent legal assistance is a necessity for a public employee retirement system, as it is for essentially all endeavors. A specific need which must be met by legal counsel is the drafting of proposed legislation when the provisions governing a system are to be amended. The lawyer reviews the proposals, studies the relationships between the proposals and existing statutes and judicial rulings, and drafts language to encompass the suggested changes. He will often be called upon to explain these changes to all interested parties and modify the language where necessary to accommodate various points of view. He may also be asked to discuss the legislation with committees of the legislature and to review amendments which may be imposed during consideration of a bill embodying the legislation.

Even where the utmost care has been taken in drafting the

---

2 See footnote 1 to Chapter 5, p. 79.

language of the laws governing the retirement system, subsequent interpretation requiring further legal help may be necessary. This is even more likely when, as is not uncommon with small systems, the provisions of some of the bills affecting a retirement system are not subject to careful legal scrutiny before enactment. In general terms, the system's lawyer must counsel the staff and board as to their responsibilities under the law. Since their actions can result in changes in benefits to participants or in other decisions which might result in law suits being brought against the system's board or staff, they need legal advice of the highest caliber.

Medical. The responsibilities of the medical advisor to a system are similar in importance to those of other technical members, but narrower in scope. The medical advisor will often be called upon to aid the system's board or staff in judgments regarding the disablement of members. He must be able to translate the technical problems of his profession, including communications with other practitioners, into language the board can understand and use.

Investment. Another type of technical advisor needed by public employee retirement systems is the professional investment counselor. The scope of his duties and his importance to the system are discussed in Chapter 7.

Outside Professional Help. In small public employee retirement systems, practical necessity dictates that all of the professional counsel be given by consultants. Larger systems may employ full-time actuaries, accountants or investment managers. A large system may still use consultants in some of these fields, either solely or to supplement its own staff. To some extent, this is done to add the knowledge and experience of the consultant to the comparable skills of the system's staff. The use of a consultant also helps to counteract the natural tendency of staff technical advisors to perpetuate existing practices for reasons of tradition and limited viewpoint. Independence is another favorable attribute of a consultant, perhaps his most important. He may perform an audit and give his report directly to the board, to give it assurance that the system's staff is properly carrying out its duties. An accounting audit is often provided through the auspices of a state or provincial auditor. Even where this occurs, an independent audit by a private accountant may be advisable, either on a regular basis or sporadically.

A somewhat different form of audit occurs in some jurisdictions where a watchdog pension commission is in existence. Such a "super-agency" might have its own staff, or employ separate consultants to analyze the reports of the retirement systems in its area. Although such a commission's audit is generally not carried out with the same degree of detail as one performed by an auditor specifically hired by the system itself, a pension commission review often puts into focus the major issues affecting public employee retirement systems. These issues include long-term financing goals, comparative investment practices, and the degree and type of uniformity of actuarial studies to be required of all the systems. This type of review can be valuable both to the general public and to the board of each system reviewed.

ADMINISTRATIVE EXPENSES

Expenses of administration are often insignificant in small public employee retirement systems. No salaries are paid directly by the system and the services provided for the system by personnel of the governmental unit may not be charged to the system by the unit. Thus the expenses for which the system is responsible may be limited to those for outside professional help and for such direct costs as bank charges and printing. These expenses would be paid either from the benefit funds of the system itself or directly by the city or other political entity controlling the system.

In larger systems, expenses are often under direct legislative control, as are the expenses of other agencies of the government. Sometimes an expense fund is developed from specifically allocated employer contributions. Occasionally the employers and participants contribute jointly to such a fund. The allocation of money from this fund for specific purposes is often subject to appropriation by the legislature as part of its budgeting process.

A number of systems meet administrative expenses out of interest earnings, in one manner or another. The interest earnings so used are those that are in excess of those required for actuarial purposes. This technique allocates administrative expenses reasonably equitably between the participants and the employers, especially where interest is credited on employee funds separately. However, in comparing a system allocating its expenses in this way with another system, care must be taken to avoid a misstatement of either the true expense costs or the true investment earnings rate. Current administrative expenses should not affect actuarial assumptions as to future rates of earnings. Similarly, except for investment counsel fees and other direct investment expenses, administrative expenses are relatively independent of fund size and earnings rate. Administrative expenses in a system with a relatively stable membership but with rapidly growing funds constitute a larger percentage of investment earnings currently than they will in the future when the fund reaches a more mature size.

BENEFITS TO PARTICIPANTS AND THEIR BENEFICIARIES

Participants are required to make regular contributions in most systems. If a participant's service is terminated, his contributions are generally returned to him, usually with interest. The rate of interest to be paid is either specified in the benefit provisions or determined by the system's investment experience. In the latter instance, the board usually has the specific responsibility for setting the rate of interest to be credited. The board thus needs accurate predictions of the investment earnings to be received until its next opportunity to review the interest crediting rate. The board must also take into account other demands upon the investment earnings of the system, particularly as they affect the actuary's determinations.

The mechanical procedures for crediting interest to each participant's account should be designed for clerical simplicity. For this reason, interest may be credited infrequently, often annually. As the use of electronic data processing equipment has become more common for this purpose, the larger systems have begun crediting interest more frequently, sometimes as often as monthly. Personnel relations are improved by this treatment because of its similarity to the more familiar treatment afforded by savings institutions. The frequent crediting of interest is at the opposite extreme from some systems' practice of not only crediting no interest in the early years of service but even confiscating some of the employee's contributions upon terminations.

In a few systems a member can borrow all or a portion of his accumulated contributions from the system. Administration of this type of arrangement can be quite difficult because of varying amounts borrowed, odd dates of borrowing, and provisions for periodic repayment of loans. The importance of the loan privilege is pointed up by the fact that new money loaned in a recent year to members of the New York State Employees' Retirement System amounted to over $40 million as compared with retirement allowances paid of somewhat less than $70 million.

The primary benefits administered by the staff of a public employee retirement system are retirement allowances. These are paid to participants who qualify because of age, service or disability, or to beneficiaries who qualify because of participants' deaths. For each benefit granted, the staff of a system must verify that the eligibility requirements are met and determine the benefit amount. This calculation is often made or reviewed by the actuary.

Payment of disability benefits imposes special demands upon an administrative staff. In many cases, the requirements for disability retirement make a clear-cut determination difficult. Moreover, periodic reviews must be made of claims that have been granted, often with an examination of each pensioner's physical condition. Many systems also provide that any workmen's compensation benefits payable are offset against the system's disability benefits, necessitating review of workmen's compensation awards. This task may be made more difficult by the commutation of such awards to single amounts, or by compromise settlements, or by other irregular payments necessitating special administrative treatment.

OTHER ADMINISTRATIVE RESPONSIBILITIES

A substantial amount of a system's staff time may be devoted to questions about persons or groups qualifying to participate in the system. For example, most systems limit participation to those meeting certain requirements as to permanence of employment. Covered positions must be either full-time or part-time with at least a specified number of hours per week or per month. Difficult interpretations requiring judgment decisions may arise because of seasonal work or because of work patterns which, although unpredictable, are close to the requirements of the system.

Many systems require a waiting period for membership, often six months or a year. The waiting period is designed to eliminate from membership the short service employee who is generally subject to a high rate of turnover. Elimination of short-term employees reduces the number of employee records that must be set up and terminated. Despite this advantage, the waiting period is not necessarily helpful administratively, particularly if data processing equipment is used. Large systems covering a number of agencies often must set up records for all employees, even for those who have not met the eligibility requirements for membership.

The records are necessary to determine the proper waiting period of an employee who has worked for more than one employer. The system may also want to remind the employer when each employee's waiting period is completed. Both of these administrative functions could be eliminated if there were no waiting period.

The administrative staff is responsible for reports submitted to federal offices for statistical purposes, to various state agencies for budgetary and informational uses, to the legislature and legislative bodies such as pension commissions, to the employers, and to the participants. Reports to employers and participants may be for the general purpose of recording the activities and progress of the system, or they may be to provide data relative to the specific employer or participant.

One staff function attaining increasing prominence in some systems is preretirement counseling. Where this service is provided, the primary responsibility of the counselor is to help each participant approaching retirement clearly understand the benefits he will obtain at retirement and the options available to him. In some systems, a significant portion of the time of the staff members having this responsibility may be devoted to matters not directly related to the system's operations. This may include review of a participant's overall financial status, suggestion of part-time activities and avocations, general discussion of medical and tax questions, and consideration of housing and travel plans after retirement. Extension of the counseling function in this way may be justified on the grounds that questions in these areas flow naturally from answers to basic questions about the system's retirement benefits.

Moreover, although some employers in a multiemployer retirement system might wish to provide this service themselves, instead of relegating it to the system's counselors, few employers have the skilled personnel with the special talents of communication required in dealing with older participants. Many employers have little interest in this aspect of their personnel relations. However it occurs, the provision of some form of general preretirement counseling is widely recognized as a means of aiding the retiree in adjusting to his new style of life.

Chapter 9

Summation

PUBLIC EMPLOYEE retirement systems are in a constant state of flux. Rare is the system that has not had some benefit change over any recent five-year period. As a result of innumerable modifications of individual systems, patterns of change are developing in benefit structure, in financing, and in other areas affecting the systems. As these patterns are emerging, so also are the controversial issues that many of them are bringing. Some of these issues are discussed in this chapter.

BENEFITS

The benefit area presents a number of major issues of current concern. Background material in this area is found in chapters 2, 3, and 4. It will be noted that none of the matters considered in this portion of the chapter is completely divorced from financing questions, even though the primary emphasis is on benefits.

Collective Bargaining. The process of collective bargaining has had an increasing effect on salaries and fringe benefits in nonfederal government employment. The formality of the negotiation procedure has advantages on both sides of the table: to labor by improving its clout, and to management by narrowing the field of those who represent the working force, with their possibly conflicting viewpoints, to whom management must listen. When an agreement is reached for a new basis of wages and benefits, a vote among the employees gives some assurance of satisfaction with the terms of the agreement. Nevertheless, the very factors which make collective bargaining advantageous to labor make it disadvantageous to the employer, who finds his negotiating position weakened to the same degree as labor's is strengthened. Moreover, the process entails hazards of specific application in the retirement area.

As benefits grow, the burden on current taxpayers of funding systems properly may prove unacceptable. This potential certainly exists in some systems covering policemen and firefighters, where the required employer contribution rates approach an amount equal to one half of payroll. Yet employees with greater bargaining strength have the ability to enforce demands for increased benefits. One of the results of such a collision of interest is that actuarial assumptions in a nominally funded system might be chosen so as to relieve the pressure. When current costs are thus understated, bargaining becomes a farce, with a false price tag attached to the benefit package. Higher benefits are granted than can be afforded, at least as measured by the current employer contribution rate. As the contingencies assumed prove to be more adverse than the assumptions, costs will climb and the extra burden will be passed on to future taxpayers. An even worse situation is where the system is unfunded and the entire cost is deferred, to be paid by future generations. In either case public employee retirement systems are in a unique and vulnerable position. Labor wants a certain increase in compensation. Management is willing to pay only a portion of labor's request currently. The difference can be compromised by making future taxpayers pay it, simply by failing to fund properly now.

Ratchet Effect. A ratchet is a wheel that can move in one direction only. The benefits of many public employee retirement systems have similar characteristics. Rules of law in some jurisdictions provide that an employee's benefits can never be lower than those in effect when he is hired. Moreover, any improvement in benefits sets a new floor below which the benefit level can never fall for employees then at work. Where this rule obtains, great care must be exercised in designing benefit improvements. If an excessive benefit is granted, it either is permanent or can be eliminated only for new employees; current employees must be given its advantages so long as they are covered by the system.

Special Benefits. Public employee retirement systems are prime targets for special benefits affecting only a small number of people. Such benefits may be granted by private bills specifically designating a person to be favored. Another technique for the same purpose is to grant special benefits to a class of employees which includes only one person or a small group of people.

A more expensive abuse is the modification of a benefit structure to provide a particular advantage to a specific individual, but in such a way that the same benefits are given to any others who happen to be in the same category. An example of this occurred in a southwestern state when a legislator asked for a change in the optional benefit he had elected under the public system of which he was a member. His request was not granted, since it would have inflicted financial hardship on the system and unfairly favored him over other employees. The legislator then forced the system to accede to his request by the simple expedient of pushing a bill to that effect through the legislature. Since the bill required the same treatment of all persons in his circumstances, others have been able to take advantage of the change in the benefits, all at an additional cost to the taxpayers.

Public employee retirement systems are particulary susceptible to this type of abuse. A large payment in cash to an individual may gain unfavorable publicity because of the evidence of immediate financial advantage. On the other hand, an equivalent windfall in retirement benefits may not require a substantial current disbursement and is less likely to reap adverse publicity. Moreover, budgetary constraints may not limit a special retirement benefit, whereas a benefit involving current disbursements might be out of the question. A particular form of special treatment which appears to prevail in many areas is the provision of disproportionate retirement benefits for legislators and other elected officials. If their retirement benefits are computed using a formula significantly more favorable than that applicable to other public employees, the cynical conclusion must be that political considerations prohibit their taking other forms of compensation which would be more immediately evident to the voter.

Employee Contributions.   Retirement systems where the employees are required to contribute have one fundamental advantage: Since the employers and employees are partners in paying for the benefits, proposals for benefit changes having excessive costs relative to their value tend to be passed by, while those of real importance to the employees are instituted and justified by the employees' willingness to pay for part of the cost. This concept presupposes the benefit improvements which require increases in employer contribution rates automatically bring increases in employee contribution rates. This is not always the case. One of the deterrents to increases in employee contribution rates in the United States is the adverse federal income tax effect. Since the employee contribution is paid from after-tax salary, there is a strong disincentive to increasing the employee contribution rate. In fact, because of the personal tax saving, an employee's take-home pay can be increased by eliminating the required employee contribution, even if the employer reduces the employee's salary by the same amount and contributes the difference as an additional employer contribution. This tax bias in favor of noncontributory systems would be eliminated if the income tax laws of the United States were to be changed to allow employees to deduct contributions to retirement plans from their taxable incomes, as can their Canadian counterparts.

An alternative to the use of employee contributions as a measure of employee acceptance of benefit improvements is to view the commitment for a retirement program as an intrinsic payroll cost. The price tag attached to a benefit improvement is then expressed in cents per hour or dollars per year, and is considered a part of the total compensation package. An improvement in retirement benefits having a certain current cost is made available by reducing wages correspondingly, or by offsetting the cost against an increase in wages which would otherwise be payable. Obviously such a concept works only if the ultimate costs are properly translated to current payroll amounts.

Younger Normal Retirement.   Chapter 5 contained a discussion of the cost of reducing the age at which an employee can retire without reduction in accrued benefits. In general, even if the average age of retirement is reduced only one or two years, the additional cost to a system can be quite significant.

In addition to the costs involved, the trend towards younger ages at normal retirement has other implications. From a sociological viewpoint, some persons find more satisfaction in work than in the leisure of retirement, particularly when they are in good health. When earlier retirement is mandatory, members of this group will be dissatisfied. Where retirement occurs at an early age, the employee may take another job and thus frustrate any effort to remove him from the labor force to make a job for a younger person. Moreover, the retirement allowance being received by the retiree may put him at an unfair advantage in obtaining a job, with adverse effects on wages in general. When such a person is receiving retirement benefits from a public employee retirement system, public acceptance of the system as a whole may suffer.

Postretirement Adjustment.   The continual erosion in the purchasing power of the dollar has focused attention on postretirement adjustments. The long term worth of the various approaches to making adjustments will be tested over the years. In one respect, widespread use of postretirement adjustment may tend to reduce resistance to inflation because so many people will be insulated from its effect. Moreover the additional consumer funds created with increased retirement allowances may be inflationary in themselves, arising as they do without a corresponding increase in the production of consumer goods.

Postretirement adjustments may also exacerbate the problems of financing retirement systems. A series of minor increases in retirement allowances can prove very expensive in the long run, as the compounding of the increases causes the total benefits to mount. For example, based on common assumptions as to mortality and interest earnings, the value of a level pension to a man retiring at age 65 is increased by over 25 percent if the pension is to be subject to a 3 percent annual increment. For a woman at the same age, the increase of value is 30 percent. The effect is more pronounced for retirements at younger ages: At age 55, the cost increases over 35 percent for a man and over 40 percent for a woman.

Despite the obvious advantages of postretirement adjustments on an automatic, continuing basis, opposition to such a procedure can be evoked from both management and labor representatives. Management's objections include the fear that the automatically increased benefits will serve as a jumping off point for demands for additional benefits, without adequate recognition being given by labor to the fact that an automatic increase in benefits represents a benefit improvement. Labor's objections include just the converse: Management may rest on its laurels, failing to recognize legitimate needs for increases beyond the automatic increase, such as when active employees receive benefit improvements or when increases in living standards outstrip the automatic increases.

Vesting. In both public and private systems, vesting and its availability are issues of continuing interest and of some controversy. Balanced against each other are the cost of vesting and the social desirability of generous vesting provisions.

One factor working to reduce the cost in public employee retirement systems is conditional vesting, vesting which can be and often is forfeited by the withdrawal of the accumulated employee contributions upon termination of employment. In the United States, over 90 percent of the nonfederal public employees covered by retirement systems make contributions under their systems; the comparable percentage for private plans is about 25 percent. Since conditional vesting exists only in contributory plans and can greatly reduce the cost of vesting, cost as a deterrent to vesting is less important in public employee retirement systems than in private plans in the United States. This could change however if a trend should develop to abandon conditional vesting in contributory programs. One way this might happen would be by voluntary amendment of benefit provisions to let terminating employees withdraw their contributions without forfeiting all of their vested benefits. Alternatively, legislation might be enacted preventing a vested employee from withdrawing his contributions; legislation of this sort is in effect in much of Canada. However brought about, such a change would be of great significance, both in increasing the costs of public employee retirement systems and in protecting their members from shortsightedly thwarting the benefit goals designed into the systems.

Benefits can also be preserved by means of reciprocal agreements between systems for the maintenance of credit for employees who transfer between the systems. However even if an employee's benefits earned with several employers are fully vested in this manner, he usually receives less in benefits than if he had stayed with one employer, owing to the tendency for the salary basis upon which his benefits are computed to be smaller with earlier employers. Although solutions to this problem have been hypothesized, the problem remains largely unsolved in practice. Professionals and other skilled employees are increasingly in demand in public employment; attractive opportunities and effective utilization of such employees will occur only if employee mobility is not discouraged. Satisfactory reciprocity arrangements could eliminate a major source of discouragement.

FINANCING AND INVESTMENT

The needs of state, provincial, and local governments for funds seem to be ever increasing. With limited resources, governments are constantly subjecting expenditures to squeezes. Public employee retirement systems are excellent starting points for those striving to achieve reduction in current expenditures. The factors which must be considered before any such reduction occurs were discussed in some detail in chapters 5, 6, and 7. These factors will be summarized below and augmented by related observations.

The Need to Know Retirement Costs. The ultimate cost of a retirement program is determined by actual benefit disbursements. However it is imperative that these costs be estimated *before* the actual disbursements are made. The cost commitment must be known when a system is established and each time thereafter that the benefit structure is modified. Further, if a wise decision is to be made about the method for meeting the costs of a retirement program, the magnitude and timing of those costs must be known.

Projections of the disbursements provide valuable information for this purpose They lack, however, two of the features of an actuarial cost method:

The ability to associate benefit improvements with current salaries, to give a measure of the worth of the improvements in current dollars;

The simplicity and ease of comparison which a level cost basis provides.

A projected cost thus goes only part way in providing the information needed for sound decisions about creating, amending, or financing a retirement system; an actuarial method of measuring the costs is required to obtain the full story. An actuarial cost method can establish prices for improvements in retirement benefits comparable to those for increases in wages and other employee compensation. These prices, in turn, should be prerequisites to negotiating benefit changes and to legislative decision making.

The taxpayer, who must ultimately pay the cost, has the right to know the cost when the commitment is being made. Perhaps a form of "truth in labeling" legislation is needed for retirement system costs. Surely taxpayers deserve the same consideration and protection as consumers or stockholders get.

Funding.   If all of the elements of cost are presented to the legislative authority and are understood, a rational decision can be made as to the amount the employer is to contribute under the retirement system. The basic arguments which might then sway the decision in favor of funding— building up a fund by paying currently accruing actuarial costs—are the following:

> Funding treats the cost of a retirement program as it really is: a payroll cost to be met currently just as are all other payroll costs, rather than to be deferred for payment by some future generation of taxpayers.
>
> The payments for funding the benefits accruing for current employees develop a pool of assets which provides assurance for those employees that their benefits will be paid when due.
>
> Funding reduces the amount of taxes to be levied, because part of the pension disbursements are met by earnings on the investments.

The first of these arguments is probably the most important. A slight restatement of it is that funding is a form of discipline. The requirement that current payroll costs be met currently avoids the expensive procrastination and wishful thinking that failure to fund can entail. Payments may be postponed under the delusion that it will be easier to pay the needed costs in the future, particularly when the problem of such future payments will be the responsibility of someone else. This approach may be politically expedient but can only create an onerous retirement system commitment for future generations.

Rate of Employer Contributions. The many variables affecting employer costs have created a wide spread in the rates of employer contributions currently in effect in the many public employee retirement systems in the United States and Canada. For example, even where the data for all of the systems of each state are combined, the employer contribution rates in a recent year ranged from a low in one state of less than 1 percent of payroll to a high in another state of nearly 15 percent. In that year, 1969, the average employer contribution for the state and local systems of the United States as a whole was 7.3 percent of salary. This rate is on an upswing since the comparable figure in 1961 was 6.5 percent. The significance of the financial commitment for public employee retirement systems can also be measured by the fact that the 1969 contribution represented 3.5 percent of the total state and local budgets.

The percentages given in the previous paragraph are based on actual employer contributions for retirement purposes. To the extent some systems are not meeting the costs of benefits currently accruing, the statistics tend to understate the true costs, which include the increase in the value of the systems' unfunded commitments. This understatement will cause future contribution rates to increase as present employees reach retirement and start receiving benefits.

Another cause of increasing employer contribution rates is the continuing liberalization of benefits. Many outcroppings of this are evident in the form of pressures for larger and earlier retirement benefits, expanded disability and survivors' benefits, increased vesting, and reduction or elimination of employee contributions. Moreover, the rapid increases in payrolls of persons covered by public employee retirement systems, to the extent that they continue in the future, will also bring higher benefits and further increase future required employer contributions.

Economic Implications. Much has been written in recent years regarding the impact of pension funds upon the overall economy. They are taking their place beside banks, savings institutions, mutual funds, and life insurance companies as major influences on the capital market. Despite the rapid increase in private pension plans in the last two decades, the older and supposedly more mature public employee retirement systems are more than holding their own in this area. In fact, in the 15-year period from 1950 to 1965, the net capital contributions of the public employee retirement systems to the capital market, when compared with the contribution of all retirement plans in the United States (excluding social security), grew from less than 18 percent to better than 26 percent.[1]

The mushrooming of public employee retirement systems can be illustrated most vividly by the figures in Table 6, which show the growth of certain financial data of all such retirement systems in the United States over a 13-year period

TABLE 6
Composite Financial Summaries of State and Local Retirement Systems in the United States (in billions)

Year	Income	Expenditures	Assets
1957	$2.5	$1.0	$12.8
1962	4.0	1.6	23.3
1967	6.6	2.7	39.3
1970	9.8	3.7	54.9

Source: U.S. Bureau of Census reports.

What does the future hold? The prognosis is for more of the same—more covered employees, more contributions, and more money in the funds. The growth rate in public employment is such as to indicate a doubling of the covered membership in public employee retirement systems in a 15-year period. A 1966 study by Daniel M. Holland, under the sponsorship of the National Bureau of Economic Research, projected total assets of U.S. public employee retirement systems in 1975 of $75 billion and in 1979 of over $100

---

[1] *Private and Public Pension Plans in the United States* (New York: Institute of Life Insurance, 1967), Table 8.

billion. Based upon the experience since the publication of his figures, even these rates of growth appear low. What is perhaps even more striking about Holland's projections is the effect he estimates public employee retirement systems will have on the capital markets in the future—the net amount which they will have for investment:

> . . . state and local funds are projected to be such powerful accumulators that by 1981 they will be buying more assets each year than industrial plans. . . . this result is uncertain, for the projections of this sector over the later years are subject to . . . error. Not open to real doubt, however, is the likelihood that state and local funds and their net purchases will continue to grow in relative importance.[2]

The size and growth potential of these funds must be given careful attention. The citizens of the United States and Canada have long been conditioned to their governments' playing major roles in economic matters, but the unique characteristics of pension funds sets them apart from most other forms of governmental expenditure. In a sense, this money is held in trust for their beneficiaries, yet they are, in another sense, at the immediate disposal of the legislative authorities governing them. Moreover, the management of these funds requires sophisticated investment skills, opening up a substantially new role for government. As the funds grow, and larger shares of the assets are held in common stocks, the proper role of government as a significant shareholder in private corporations will need to be considered most carefully.[3]

GENERAL

Some of the issues facing those responsible for public employee retirement systems are of a broad scope, affecting

---

[2] Daniel M. Holland, *Private Pension Funds: Projected Growth* (New York: National Bureau of Economic Research, 1966).

[3] For a thorough analysis of the role of pension funds in the economic scene, and some provocative philosophical implications, see Paul T. Harbrecht, S.J., *Pension Funds and Economic Power* (New York: The Twentieth Century Fund, 1959).

benefit structure, financing and all other aspects of the public retirement scene. The balance of this chapter will be devoted to three of these.

Social Security.   In the United States, public employees at both the federal and nonfederal levels make up the only large group not covered under either social security or the Railroad Retirement Act. At the state and local level, social security coverage is dependent on an interaction of federal enablement and local acceptance by referendum voting. As a result, about two thirds of the state and local employees are covered by social security and about one third are not. The units covered change occasionally, as new groups join and others leave.

A major factor causing groups to abandon social security coverage and others not to participate is the cost of the program. Comparisons have been prepared which purport to demonstrate that comparable retirement benefits could be obtained more cheaply by making arrangements outside social security. Analysis of these comparisons requires a high level of sophistication, because of the importance of the assumptions used in the comparisons and the complex nature of the social security program. The choice of interest rate to be used in the comparison is critical, since a rate too low will underestimate the benefits that can be accrued by accumulating money in a local fund rather than making equivalent contributions under social security. Incomplete comparisons can result from failure to include the ancillary benefits (e.g., death and disability) of the social security program or to recognize the likely growth in social security benefits from their present level because of increases in wage and price levels. To emphasize the importance of the latter point, Wilbur D. Mills, chairman of the House Committee on Ways and Means, projects the maximum benefits for a worker and his spouse in the year 2000 to be about $1,200 a month, as compared with a corresponding maximum monthly benefit of $443 in 1971.[4] In each case, the benefit is the amount

---

4 From a speech prepared for delivery July 28, 1971, to the National Conference of State Social Security Administrators.

payable for persons who work for a lifetime under the law's maximum salary provisions.

Nevertheless, some systems may be able to reduce the total employer and employee financial commitment by providing their members benefits similar to those the members lose by not being covered by social security. The savings in cost can arise because of:

> Artificially high benefits paid under social security for residual or supplementary credits earned by members not currently covered by social security;
>
> Individual characteristics of the group which would make it more likely to pay more in aggregate in social security taxes than would be received in benefits;
>
> Inability to match the automatic vesting and reciprocity features of social security.

When a group withdraws from social security, many of its members are "fully insured" under social security because of their past covered service. They thus retain rights to receive some social security benefits. Those who have not accrued such rights may still earn partial social security coverage by moonlighting[5] or by switching to covered employment after retiring from a public system. The latter route to social security benefits among employees otherwise not covered is a relatively simple one to follow for the many employees, especially policemen and firefighters, who can retire from public employment before age 60. No matter how a person earns partial social security coverage, his average wages and therefore his benefits for social security purposes are smaller than they would be if all his employment had been under social security. Even in this respect, though, he gets favorable treatment under social security. This is because social security benefits for low-paid employees are equal to a relatively high percentage of covered earnings. An employee who switches to covered employment after retiring from a public employee retirement system also benefits by the social secu-

---

5 See footnote 15, p. 75.

rity provision allowing a dropout of the five years of his lowest earnings in the calculation of his benefits. This dropout prevents his average wage from being dragged down by five of his years without earnings under social security. In many ways, then, employees not covered by social security may use the provisions of social security law to their advantage. The contributions saved by not being under social security may be translated into better benefits in the local system covering the employees. If so, it is entirely possible for many such employees to obtain a greater overall benefit than if their public employment were covered by social security, although the advantages of this approach will not be uniformly spread among all such employees.

Self-insurance might also be cheaper than social security in a predominantly young group, very few of whose members will receive the advantages of benefits in the near future after minimal contributions. Similarly, a group made up primarily of women teachers is sometimes said to receive less in benefits than their social security taxes buy because the survivorship benefits are of essentially no value to the single women, or else the married women are already entitled to substantial benefits from their husbands' social security. However this cannot be categorically stated, since women at retirement also get more for their money than men, due to their longer life expectancy. Moreover, any comparison of the cost advantages of an individual group may be valid only temporarily, due both to changes in the group's average age and service characteristics and to changes in the social security laws which might alter the comparisons for any particular group.

Since social security covers most of the working population of the United States, the accrued benefits of any individual continue to grow as he moves from job to job in covered employment. However, when a person moves to a job that is not covered by social security, this accrual stops growing and may well decline. A program in a public employee retirement system which attempts to emulate social security will have a similar failing for employees transferring out of the system without vested benefits. However the loss of benefits is much more likely in a public system, because change of employment so often moves a person outside the particular system but so rarely moves a person covered by social security to a job not covered. For this reason, the system's costs would tend to be lower than social security's because of the forfeited benefits of those employees who do not remain in the system long enough to acquire vested benefits. With the widespread attention being focused upon vesting and portability of benefits, this saving in cost would seem of questionable value when balanced against the reduced retirement benefits which bring it about. In fact, the social advantages of universal social security coverage would seem to outweigh any of the financial advantages which might result from keeping public employees out of social security. Until federal employees are also covered, however, this last argument on philosophical grounds would seem idle.

A strong incentive to include all employees under social security would occur if a portion of the cost of social security were borne out of general tax revenues. Proposals to this effect have been discussed from time to time, with the general concept being that one third of the cost would be carried by the government through general tax revenues, the balance being shared in equal proportion by employers and employees. If this approach were adopted, the employee who is not covered by social security would nevertheless be contributing through his income tax payments to the financing of its benefits. This would certainly encourage public employee groups to join social security or stay in, by making the benefits to be received much more attractive when compared to the employer and employee contributions to be paid.[6]

Conglomerates. The advantages enjoyed by larger systems, as noted in Chapter 2,[7] have led to the gradual centralizing of systems within states and provinces. Small systems

---

[6] For additional comments on this topic, see Paul H. Jackson, "Future of Social Security Benefits and their Impact on Integrated Plans," *Public Employee Retirement Administration* (Municipal Finance Officers Association), 1968, p. 13.

[7] See p. 20.

tend to be combined into one or two larger systems. This has been particularly true for policemen and firefighters, for whom a number of states have replaced individual systems with combined statewide systems. A common advantage of such a change is the establishment of a level contribution rate statewide, one which does not increase or decrease as freely as corresponding rates do in smaller systems. The change may also result in the state or province taking a financial part in meeting the obligations of the system, the legislature thus being responsible for meeting part of the costs of benefits which it has often caused to exist.

Probably the greatest problem of the very large systems is their concentration of political power. Each of them invests millions of dollars each month and has the potential of bringing an increasingly large bloc of voters (their active and retired participants) to bear on issues. The emerging of these systems as political forces is too recent to be analyzed in any depth, but their performance bears watching in the next several years.

Public Pension Commissions.   As the task of legislative management of public employee retirement systems becomes more complex, many states have established watchdog committees to advise on public employee pension matters. These are generally branches of the legislatures. Their function is to review the activities of the various systems within their jurisdictions and screen legislative proposals.

The decisions of a public pension commission must have credibility and be respected in the legislature, if the commission is to be effective. Ideally, a legislature will not consider a bill affecting public employee pensions unless the measure has been reviewed by the pension commission. For such a review to be meaningful, the commission must require that the cost of all proposals be obtained and made public. Further, the commission should have the experience and sophistication to be able to look behind each bill and seek out additional data where the bill has far-reaching implications. The report to the legislature on any measure should bring out all of the issues involved in a clear fashion so that all legislators, including those who are not skilled in pension matters, will be able to make a reasoned judgment. If the pension commission has gained the respect of the legislature, the legislature will refuse to act without such guidelines and ill-considered legislation will be thwarted.

Appendix A

Glossary

Occasionally one of the words or phrases contained in this glossary will be used in a context which will cause it to have a somewhat different meaning than that given below. For example, the phrase *public employee retirement system,* as used in this book, excludes federal plans; elsewhere the term may or may not be so limited. The text will often amplify the meaning of a term. The index should be consulted for any word or phrase requiring additional definition.

A glossary containing additional pension terms of general usage has been published by the Accounting Principles Board of the American Institute of Certified Public Accountants as Appendix B of its *Accounting for the Cost of Pension Plans* (New York, 1966). This may be supplemented by reference to the terms approved by the Committee on Pension and Profit Sharing Terminology as a result of a joint undertaking of the Pension Research Council and the Committee on Insurance Terminology of the American Risk and Insurance Association. Definitions of terms arising commonly in public employee retirement system operations will be found in a publication of the Municipal Finance Officers Association entitled *Public Employee Retirement Terminology* (Chicago, 1956).

Accrued Benefit Cost Method—The accrued benefit cost method (sometimes called the unit credit cost method) is one of the actuarial cost methods. Actuarial costs under this method are based directly on benefits accrued to the date of cost determination, as determined either by the terms of the benefit program or by some assumed allocation of total benefits to years of service.

Accrued Benefit Funding Method—The accrued benefit funding method is a funding method analogous to the accrued benefit cost method.

Actuarial Assumptions—Actuarial assumptions are those used in actuarial calculations to forecast uncertain future events or experience.

Actuarial Cost—A cost is characterized as actuarial if it is derived through the use of present values. An actuarial cost is often used to associate the costs of benefits under a retirement system with the approximate time the benefits are earned.

Actuarial Cost Method—An actuarial cost method is a particular technique for establishing the amount and incidence of the actuarial cost of retirement system benefits, or benefits and expenses, and the related actuarial liabilities.

Actuarial Equivalent—An actuarial equivalent is a benefit having the same present value as the benefit it replaces.

Actuarial Gains and Losses—An actuarial gain or loss is either an *actuarial experience gain or loss* or an *actuarial revaluation gain or loss.*

Actuarial Experience Gains and Losses—Actuarial experience gains or losses are the effects on actuarial costs of deviations between the past events predicted by actuarial assumptions and the events that actually occurred.

Actuarial Liability—The actuarial liability of a retirement system at any time is the excess of the present value of all benefits thereafter payable under the system over the present value of future normal costs.

Actuarial Revaluation Gains and Losses—Actuarial revaluation gains or losses are the effects on actuarial costs of adopting different actuarial cost methods or making changes in actuarial assumptions as to future events.

Ad Hoc (Postretirement Adjustment)—An ad hoc postretirement adjustment is one establishing a schedule of nonrecurring increases in retirement allowances.

Age Retirement—Age retirement is normal retirement dependent upon attainment of a specified age.

Annual Supplemental Cost—The annual supplemental cost for a given year is the portion of the supplemental cost and interest on it allocated to such year.

Annuity—An annuity is a series of periodic payments, usually for life, payable monthly or at other specified intervals. The term is frequently used to describe the part of a retirement allowance derived from a participant's contributions. Compare Pension.

Annuity Conversion Rate—An annuity conversion rate is a factor used to determine the amount of annuity payable for each dollar of a participant's contributions accumulated to the date of retirement. Annuity conversion rates generally vary by age and sex.

Antiselection—Antiselection is the tendency of a person to recognize his health status in selecting the option under a retirement system which is most favorable to himself. In insurance usage the term generally refers to the tendency of a person in an impaired health status to apply for an insurance contract favorable to himself and detrimental to the insurance company.

Automatic (Postretirement Adjustment)—An automatic postretirement adjustment is a program providing for recurring adjustments in retirement allowances on a regular basis.

Bond-swapping—Bond-swapping is a method of valuing bonds which are purchased to replace similar bonds of lower yield. Bond-swapping minimizes the reduction in bond book values which might otherwise occur with sales and purchases at prices below par.

Canada Pension Plan—The Canada Pension Plan is one of the social security programs in Canada. See Social Security.

Career Average Salary—Career average salary is that measure of a participant's level of earnings which is based on his entire period of service with a retirement system. A participant's career average salary may be one of the factors used in determining the amount of his benefits.

Conditional Vesting—Conditional vesting is that form of vesting under which entitlement to a vested benefit is conditional upon the nonwithdrawal of the participant's contributions.

Conglomerate System—A conglomerate system is one encompassing several governmental units, such as the cities and towns of a state.

Consumer Price Index—The consumer price index is the name given in both the United States and Canada to the series of numbers whose ratios measure the relative prices at various times of a selected group of goods and services which typify those bought by urban families.

Contributory—A retirement system is contributory if its members must aid in its financing by making periodic contributions, usually as a payroll deduction.

Cost of Living—Cost of living is the average cost of the goods and services required by a person or family. Compare Living Standard.

Current Disbursement Cost Method—The current disbursement cost method (sometimes called pay-as-you-go) is a method of recognizing the costs of a retirement system only as benefits are paid.

Defined Benefit—A benefit program uses defined benefits if benefits to be received by employees after retirement are predetermined by a formula. The employer's contributions under such a program are determined on the basis of the benefits which are thus payable.

Defined Contribution—A benefit program uses defined contributions when the rate of contribution of the employer (or employee) is fixed and the benefits to be received by employees after retirement are dependent to some extent upon such contributions. The type of defined contribution program most common among public employee retirement systems is the money purchase benefit program.

Disability Retirement—Disability retirement is a termination of employment, generally involving the payment of a retirement allowance, as a result of an accident or sickness occurring before a participant is eligible for normal retirement.

Early Retirement—Early retirement is a termination of employment involving the payment of a retirement allowance before a participant is eligible for normal retirement. The retirement allowance payable in the event of early retirement is often lower than the accrued portion of the normal retirement allowance.

Entry-Age Normal Cost Method—See Projected Benefit Cost Method.

Equity Annuity—An equity annuity (sometimes called a variable annuity) is a benefit whose payments vary from year to year depending upon the value of a portfolio of securities (usually common stocks).

Final Average Salary—Final average salary is that measure of a participant's level of earnings which is based on his average rate of salary for a specified period of time, usually the 3, 5, or 10 years immediately preceding retirement. A participant's final average salary may be one of the factors used in determining the amount of his benefits.

Funding—Funding is a systematic program under which assets are set aside in amounts and at times approximately coincident with the accruing of benefit rights under a retirement system.

Leapfrogging—Leapfrogging is the practice by each of two or more retirement systems (often in the same state or province) of obtaining in rotation better benefits for its members than those of the other systems.

Living Standard—Living standard is a measure of the average cost of goods and services consumed by a person or family. Living standard differs from cost of living in recognizing the changes in consumption which arises from increases in wages and productivity.

Mechanism (of Postretirement Adjustment)—The mechanism of a program of postretirement adjustments is the technique used to determine the amount of the adjustment. The mechanism may involve a formula which is based on salaries, investment yields, or other indexes.

Member—See Participant.

Modified Refund Annuity—A modified refund annuity is a form of retirement allowance which provides a benefit upon the death of a retired employee equal to the excess, if any, of the amount of his own contributions over the total retirement allowance payments he received prior to his death.

Money Purchase—A money purchase benefit program is a type of defined contribution benefit program. Under such a program, the employer's or employee's contributions are usually accumulated to the employee's benefit and the retirement benefit payable to him is the actuarial equivalent of the sum so accumulated.

Noncontributory—A retirement system is noncontributory if no contributions are required of its members to aid in its financing.

Normal Cost—Normal cost is the cost assigned under an actuarial cost method to any year after the inception of a retirement system. Normal cost does not include any portion of the supplemental cost, but may include adjustments for actuarial experience gains or losses.

Normal Retirement—Normal retirement is a termination of employment involving the payment of a regular formula retirement allowance without reduction because of age or service and without special qualifications such as disability.

Normal Retirement Date—The normal retirement date is the earliest date at which a participant qualifies for normal retirement.

OASDHI—OASDHI means Federal Old-Age and Survivors Disability, and Health Insurance, the social security program in the United States. See Social Security.

Old Age Security Plan—The Old Age Security Plan is one of the social security programs in Canada. See Social Security.

Participant—A participant (sometimes called a member) in a retirement system is an employee or former employee who may become eligible to receive or is receiving benefits under the system.

Pay-as-you-go—See Current Disbursement Cost Method.

Pension—A pension is a series of periodic payments, usually for life, payable monthly or at other specified intervals. The term is frequently used to describe the part of a retirement allowance financed by employer contributions. Compare Annuity.

Political Subdivision—A political subdivision of a state or province is a lower governmental unit, such as a city, county, school district, or utility district.

Postretirement Adjustment—A postretirement adjustment is a change (usually an increase) in the amount of a retirement allowance after its commencement to reflect changes or anticipated changes in cost of living or living standards.

Present Value—The present value (sometimes called actuarial present value) of an amount or series of amounts payable or receivable in the future is their current worth after discounting each such amount at an assumed rate of interest and adjusting for the probability of its payment or receipt.

Prior Service Cost—A prior service cost is a type of supplemental cost arising under some actuarial cost methods because of benefits provided for service prior to the establishment of a retirement system.

Projected Benefit Cost Method—The projected benefit cost method (sometimes called the entry-age normal cost method) is one of the actuarial cost methods. Actuarial costs under this method are based upon total prospective benefits, whether or not they are associated with any specific periods of service. The actuarial cost determination assumes regular future accruals of normal cost, generally in a level amount or percentage of earnings.

Projected Benefit Funding Method—The projected benefit funding method is a funding method analogous to the projected benefit cost method.

Public Employee Retirement System—A public employee retirement system is an organization providing a formal program of retirement benefits for employees of states, provinces, or their political subdivisions.

Quebec Pension Plan—The Quebec Pension Plan is one of the social security programs in Canada. It is comparable to the Canada Pension Plan, with which it is closely coordinated. The Quebec Pension Plan operates in the province of Quebec; the Canada Pension Plan operates in the rest of Canada. See Social Security.

Ratchet Effect—The ratchet effect is the result of a legal prohibition, often constitutional in nature, against a legislative body's reducing the rights of a participant to benefits under a public employee retirement system.

Refund Annuity—A refund annuity is a form of retirement allowance which provides a benefit upon the death of a retired employee equal to the excess, if any, of the amount of his own contributions over the total annuity payments (derived from these contributions) he received prior to his death.

Retirement Allowance—A retirement allowance is a series of payments, usually for life, payable monthly or at other specified intervals. The term is used to describe the entire benefit payable, including both the annuity derived from the participant's accumulated contributions and the pension financed by the employer's contributions.

Scope (of Postretirement Adjustment)—The scope of a program of postretirement adjustments defines the program's applicability (as to persons and benefits) and whether the adjustments are *ad hoc,* automatic, or both.

Service Retirement—Service retirement is normal retirement dependent upon completion of a specified period of service. In some usages, the term has the same meaning as *normal retirement.*

Social Security—Social security is a federal program of old-age and related benefits covering most workers in the country. In the United States, social security benefits are provided by OASDHI. In Canada they arise from the Old Age Security Plan (which provides benefits for essentially all old-age persons) and the Canada and Quebec Pension Plans (which cover workers and their families) .

Spouse's Benefit—A spouse's benefit (sometimes called a widow's benefit) is a retirement allowance payable to the spouse of a participant following his death before retirement.

Supplemental Cost—A supplemental cost is a separate element of actuarial cost which results from future normal costs having a present value less than the present value of the total prospective benefits of the system. Such supplemental cost is generally the result of assuming that actuarial costs accrued before the establishment of the system. A supplemental cost may also arise after inception of the system because of benefit changes, changes in actuarial assumptions, actuarial losses, or failure to fund or otherwise recognize normal cost accruals or interest on supplemental cost.

Thirteenth Check—A thirteenth check is an annual supplemental retirement allowance arising from earnings on the investments of a system in excess of those determined as needed for other purposes.

Unfunded Actuarial Liability—The unfunded actuarial liability (sometimes called the unfunded liability) of a retirement system at any time is the excess of its actuarial liability at that time over the value of its cash and investments.

Unit Credit Cost Method—See Accrued Benefit Cost Method.

Variable Annuity—See Equity Annuity.

Vested Benefits—Vested benefits are those whose payment is not contingent upon a participant's continuation in specified employment.

Widow's Benefit—See Spouse's Benefit.

Withdrawal—Withdrawal is the termination of employment prior to becoming eligible for any benefits. The term sometimes refers to subsequent termination of membership in a system by withdrawal of the employee's available accumulated contributions from the system.

Appendix B

Excerpts from Booklet Describing the California Public Employees' Retirement System

INTRODUCTION

EMPLOYEES of the State of California have enjoyed a system of retirement, disability, and death benefits since 1931. In 1939 the system was extended to public agencies in California on a contractual basis. Each year the legislature makes many changes in the laws pertaining to the system. One of the most important changes was enacted in 1971, when the long-standing "1/60th formula" for miscellaneous employees was changed to a "1/50th" (or 2 percent) formula.

This booklet is intended to provide a general discussion of the benefits available as of July, 1971. Since the explanation must be general, this booklet is informative only.

The statements in this booklet are general and simplified as much as possible, consistent with accuracy. The law is both specific and detailed. Regardless of any inferences any reader may draw, the law must be obeyed. If there is any conflict, the law takes precedence.

All numerical values have also been generalized and, where possible, simplified so as to enable the typical employee to make a close estimate of the factors that affect him. However, only a review of your record can determine the exact facts in any individual case.

MEMBERSHIP

PERS members fall into two classes—"miscellaneous members" and "safety members." A safety member, very generally, is an employee engaged in the maintenance of law, fire suppression, or activities in which disorder may be an important factor. All other members, the majority, are "miscellaneous members," for whom this booklet is primarily intended.

Virtually all employees become members of PERS when they are hired. Most of the exceptions are those who work less than half time. There are exceptions, however, even to the exceptions. Under many conditions, membership in the system continues even though employment is not continuous or with the same employer.

If there is any doubt, ask your supervisor or appointing official.

In addition to becoming a member of PERS on the date of your appointment, you will probably be covered under the Federal Social Security System. If you are not certain, ask your employer.

Excepting for a minor adjustment to your retirement benefits, described later in this booklet, the two systems are independent.

While a member of PERS you will receive a yearly statement of retirement contributions, interest earned, and years of service credited to your account.

Information pertinent to your Social Security account can be obtained only through application to the Social Security Administration.

CONTRIBUTIONS

PERS is a funded system; in other words, the money is on deposit to meet obligations when they come due. The funds derive from three sources—your contributions, employer contributions, and earnings from investments.

The money you contribute is yours. It is earmarked in an individual account that draws interest at a rate established periodically by the PERS Board of Administration. If you leave before retirement age and do not take a job with an agency that is covered by the PERS system, you can have your money refunded, with interest. The contributions of your employer, however, will not be refunded.

Your contribution will be 7% of your gross pay. If you are covered by Social Security the 7% will apply to only a part of your pay. The law states that only ⅔ of the normal contribution rate will apply to the first $400 of your monthly pay. Since ⅔ of $400 is 266.67, the net effect is the same as if your gross pay minus $133.33 was multiplied by 7%.

Refund of Contributions. If you leave state and other covered agency service before reaching retirement age, either to take a job with an employer who is not covered by the system or to remain at home, your contributions may be refunded with earned interest. If you have a total of five years of credited service with one or more employers covered by PERS you have the right to leave your contributions on deposit in return for a retirement allowance when you reach retirement age.

If you have worked for less than five years, your contributions, with earned interest, must be refunded to you in a lump sum.

Interest is paid to the last day of the preceding fiscal year. Contributions withdrawn as of July 1 will, therefore, receive all accumulated interest. Those withdrawn as of June 29 would, in effect, lose a year's interest. As of July 1, 1971 the interest rate credited to employee accounts was 4¾%.

RETIREMENT BENEFITS

The retirement benefit structure administered by PERS is very simple, but the exceptions, modifications, and options to the basic formula can be complex and subtle. Remember, therefore, that this pamphlet can be used for estimating your retirement benefits, but only an analysis of your records by a qualified Retirement Officer can establish the exact amount of your benefits.

The "normal" retirement age, upon which all calculations are based, is 60. Minimum retirement age is 55. At present the mandatory retirement age is 70. As of October 1, 1971, this will drop to age 69. On October 1, 1972 the mandatory age will drop to age

68. On October 1, 1973, the mandatory age will drop to age 67, where it will remain. Eligibility for retirement before the compulsory retirement age is reached, requires at least five years of service credit.

Retirement at the mandatory age must take effect on the first of the month following the date at which a member reaches such age.

The basic formula of "1/50th at age 60" makes for easy estimation of retirement benefits. Since 1/50th is 2%, multiplication of the number of years of credited service times 2% times monthly pay gives the amount you will receive as an unmodified allowance if you retire at age 60.

The monthly pay used in this calculation will be the average pay earnable during the last 3 years of service, unless the member notifies the system of a consecutive three-year period during which his pay was higher. This figure is referred to as "final compensation."

The retirant at age 60 who has 10 years of credited service will have an unmodified allowance of 20% of his final compensation. For 20 years he will have 40%; for thirty years he will have 60%.

TABLE B-1
Estimated Service Retirement Allowance as a Percentage of Final Compensation* (2% at 60 formula benefits, male members)

Years' Service	Age at Retirement								
	55	56	57	58	59	60	61	62	63 and Older
10	14.1	15.1	16.2	17.3	18.6	20.0	21.3	22.7	24.2
15	21.2	22.7	24.2	26.0	27.9	30.0	32.0	34.1	36.3
20	28.2	30.2	32.3	34.7	37.2	40.0	42.7	45.4	48.4
25	35.3	37.8	40.4	43.4	46.6	50.0	53.4	56.8	60.5
30	42.4	45.3	48.5	52.0	55.9	60.0	64.0	68.2	72.5
35	49.4	52.9	56.6	60.7	65.2	70.0	74.7	79.5	84.6

* Highest average monthly compensation earnable by a member during any period of three consecutive years during his membership in the System.

		Examples—Male Employee	Your Case
1. Age at retirement	59	64	
2. Total service to retirement	25 yrs	35 yrs.	yrs.
3. Final compensation	$600.00	$800.00	$
4. 2% at 60 benefit as percent of compensation	46.6%	84.6%	%
5. Amount of 2% at 60 benefit (line 3 times line 4)	$279.60	$676.80	$

At ages other than 60, there are reductions and augmentations. If you retire before age 60 your unmodified allowance will be reduced; if you retire after age 60 it will be augmented. The augmentation increases with each year of age up to age 63. After that age the augmentation factor remains constant.

The percentages of final compensation payable as an unmodified allowance at selected ages and number of years of service are shown in Tables B-1 and B-2. Note that the percentages differ slightly for males and females; use the appropriate table in finding the value that applies to you.

TABLE B-2
Estimated Service Retirement Allowance as a Percentage of Final Compensation* (2% at 60 formula benefits, female members)

Years' Service	Age at Retirement								
	55	56	57	58	59	60	61	62	63 and Older
10	14.6	15.5	16.5	17.6	18.7	20.0	21.3	22.6	24.0
15	21.9	23.3	24.8	26.4	28.1	30.0	31.9	33.9	36.0
20	29.2	31.0	33.0	35.2	37.5	40.0	42.6	45.2	48.0
25	36.5	38.8	41.3	44.0	46.9	50.0	53.2	56.6	60.0
30	43.8	46.6	49.5	52.7	56.2	60.0	63.8	67.9	72.0
35	51.1	54.3	57.8	61.5	65.6	70.0	74.5	79.2	84.0

* Highest average compensation earnable by a member during any period of three consecutive years during her membership in the System.

MODIFIED BASIC FORMULA

Most employees who are PERS members are now covered under Social Security. The formula for calculating retirement benefits for members under coordinated coverage must, therefore, be modified to take account of this fact. Under the formula, the full, unmodified allowance, is reduced for the period of service covered by Social Security.

Table B-3 shows the dollar reduction in the unmodified allowance (which you've just figured from Table B-1 or B-2) for coordinated coverage with Social Security. Notice that Table B-3 is in terms of dollars, whereas Tables B-1 and B-2 are in percentages.

TABLE B-3
Approximate Dollar Reduction in Unmodified Allowance for Members Coordinated with Social Security (based on $400 monthly minimum earning, male and female)

Years' Service under Social Security	Age at Retirement								
	55	56	57	58	59	60	61	62	63 and Older
10	18.83	20.13	21.55	23.12	24.83	26.67	28.45	30.29	32.24
15	28.24	30.20	32.32	34.68	37.24	40.00	42.68	45.44	48.36
20	37.65	40.27	43.09	46.24	49.65	53.33	56.91	60.59	64.48
25	47.07	50.33	53.87	57.80	62.07	66.67	71.13	75.73	80.60
30	56.48	60.40	64.64	69.36	74.48	80.00	85.36	90.88	96.72
35	65.89	70.47	75.41	80.92	86.89	93.33	99.59	106.03	112.84

Example: Male employee—Suppose your "final compensation" is $600. You plan to retire at age 64 and will have 30 years of credited service at that age. Your retirement is coordinated with Social Security and you will have a total of 10 years service under Social Security by the time you retire.

	Example	*Your Case*
1. Age at retirement	64	
2. Total service at retirement	30 years	
3. Final compensation	$600 per month	
4. Benefit per Table B-1		
(72.5% x $600)	$435.00	
5. Reduction per Table B-3		
(10 years of Social Security) ...	$ 32.24	
6. Unmodified monthly allowance	$402.76	

Cost of Living Adjustment.   Provision for an annual "cost of living" adjustment to retirement allowances was incorporated into the retirement law in 1968.

On April 1st of each year, each account is adjusted to reflect the change, if any, in the California Consumer Price Index. In practice, this is taken as the average of the Los Angeles-Long Beach and San Francisco-Oakland area cost of living indices, published by the Bureau of Labor Statistics of the United States Department of Labor. The adjustment is subject to the following limitations:

1. No adjustment will be made in years for which the adjustment to the member's base allowance would be less than 1%. "Base allowance" is the member's monthly allowance minus accumulated cost of living increases already granted.
2. Allowances may not be reduced below the base allowance.
3. Increases will commence in the second calendar year following the year of retirement and may not exceed 2% per year, compounded from the base year. The "base year" is the year of retirement.

4. The increase applies to nearly all members and beneficiaries receiving a monthly allowance from the System.
It *does not* apply to benefits payable under the 1959 Survivor Allowance or to the basic death benefit.

The member does not have to apply for these increases. They are calculated and granted automatically, and appear, when applicable, in the May 1st allowance payment.

TABLE B-4
Temporary Annuity to Age 62 or 65* (reduction of monthly life income from the retirement system for each $10.00 of the temporary monthly annuity payments)

	Temporary Annuity to:			
	Age 62		*Age 65*	
	Male	*Female*	*Male*	*Female*
55	$4.81	$4.11	$6.40	$5.47
56	4.30	3.67	6.01	5.12
57	3.75	3.18	5.58	4.73
58	3.14	2.65	5.11	4.31
59	2.47	2.07	4.58	3.85
60	1.72	1.44	4.00	3.35
61	0.90	0.75	3.36	2.80

* Applies only to members whose employment was covered under Social Security.
The temporary annuity is not available if the member on the date of retirement is entitled to receive Social Security Program benefits.

Example: A male employee who is covered under Social Security retires at age 60 with an unmodified life allowance of $250 from the Retirement System. He is "fully insured" under Social Security and his estimated primary Social Security benefit will provide an additional monthly income of $100.00 if he waits until 65 to begin receiving it. He elects to take the temporary annuity payments to age 65. At age 60, his monthly life income will be reduced by $4.00 for each $10.00 of temporary annuity payments to age 65. His $250 allowance will be reduced by a total of $40.00 ($4.00 times 10) to $210.00. The Retirement System would then pay a total of $310.00 ($210.00 plus $100) until he reaches age 65, at which time his System allowance would be reduced to $210.00 for the remainder of his life. He can now, however, begin receiving his Social Security benefit.

Temporary Annuity Payment. Should you elect to retire before Social Security payments can begin, you may elect to take a *temporary annuity payment.* Under this plan, your allowance will be converted into a reduced life allowance, which is somewhat less than the unmodified allowance. To this life allowance, will be added the estimated monthly sum you will receive from Social Security when you reach age 62 or 65. At that age, when Social Security payments begin, the Retirement System will continue to pay you only the reduced life allowance. The plan, in effect, provides you with a higher income than you would otherwise have received at the time of retirement before age 62, thus encouraging early retirement for those who could not otherwise afford to do so.

Table B-4, and the example, illustrate this plan.

OPTIONS

The unmodified allowance ceases at the death of the retired member. Four options, the chief purpose of which is to protect survivors, are available. The first three are exercised by a great many, the fourth being used only in special cases. Each option reduces the amount of the unmodified allowance, in return for benefits after the retired member's death.

Option No. 1: Option No. 1 guarantees that the retired member's contributions and interest will be returned to his beneficiary, if the retired member dies before they are disbursed.

Table B-5
Option No. I—Reduction in Unmodified Allowance for Each $1,000 of Employee's Accumulated Contributions

Age at Retirement	Male	Female
55	$0.84	$0.52
60	1.05	.63
65	1.38	.81
70	1.91	1.12

	Example: Male Employee	Your Case
1. Age at retirement	60	
2. 2% unmodified allowance (from Table B-1)	$ 279.60	$
3. Estimated contributions at retirement	$4,000.00	$
4. Option 1 reduction factor	$ 1.05	$
5. Reduction .... 1.05 x 4 =	$ 4.20	$
6. Option 1 monthly allowance	$ 275.40	$

Since a portion of the monthly allowance is purchased by employer contributions, the member's account diminishes by considerably less than the monthly benefit paid him. The remainder of the member's account, if there is any, will be paid to the survivor either in a lump sum or monthly payments.

In return for this "insurance," there is a slight reduction in monthly benefits. Table B-5 shows the amount of reduction (the premium) for this option at various ages at retirement. The example will show you how to figure your premium.

Option No. 2: This option provides for a reduced income during the life of the retired member, with the same amount continuing for the life of the beneficiary named at the time of retirement. For a table of reductions, see Table B-6.

TABLE B-6
Option No. 2—Percentage of Unmodified Allowance Payable to Male Member with Same Amount to Continue to Female Beneficiary

Age of Female Beneficiary	Age of Retiring Member			
	55	60	65	70
50	76.4	69.7	62.0	53.3
55	79.5	73.0	65.3	56.4
60	82.8	76.7	69.3	60.2
65	86.2	80.8	73.8	65.0
70	89.5	85.0	78.9	70.5

Example: Male employee—Suppose that you are retiring at age 65 with an unmodified monthly retirement allowance of $300. Your wife, who is your beneficiary, is age 60. You elect to take Option No. 2. A male employee retiring at age 65 with a female beneficiary, age 60, would receive 69.3% of his unmodified retirement allowance under this option.

69.3% of $300 = $207.90, your Option No. 2 monthly allowance. If you should die before your wife, this same amount would be paid to her for the rest of her life.

TABLE B-7
Option No. 3—Percentage of Unmodified Allowance Payable to Male Member with One-Half (½) the Amount to Continue to Female Beneficiary

Age of Female Beneficiary	Age of Retiring Male Member			
	55	60	65	70
50	86.6	82.2	76.6	69.5
55	88.6	84.4	79.0	72.1
60	90.6	86.8	81.8	75.2
65	92.6	89.4	84.9	78.8
70	94.5	91.9	88.2	82.7

Example: Male employee—Suppose that you are retiring at age 65 with an unmodified monthly retirement allowance of $300. Your wife, who is your beneficiary, is age 60. You elect to take Option No. 3. A male employee retiring at age 65 with a female beneficiary, age 60, would receive 81.8% of his unmodified retirement allowance under this option.

81.8% of $300 = $245.40, your Option No. 3 monthly allowance. If you should die before your wife, one-half (½) of this amount or $122.70 would be paid to her for the rest of her life.

Option No. 3: This option provides for a reduced income during the life of the retired member, with the beneficiary named at the time of retirement receiving *one-half* the amount of the annuitant's allowance after the death of the retired member. Because the survivor will receive a smaller allowance, the allowance paid to the retired member during his life is larger than under Option No. 2. Table B-7 shows the effect of this option.

Option No. 4: A member, at retirement, may elect, with the approval of the Board of Administration, to receive such other joint life benefits as are the actuarial equivalent of his retirement allowance. This option is exercised very seldom. It is provided for those few special cases not satisfied by any of the three standard options.

OTHER BENEFITS

In addition to service retirement benefits, your retirement system provides other benefits. Among these are disability benefits, death benefits, and survivor benefits.

Disability Benefits. If, through injury or illness, you cannot perform the duties of your position and if you have five or more years of credited service you *may* be eligible for a monthly disability allowance. The factors used in computing disability allowances are final compensation and years of service.

Unlike the service retirement, however, there are provisions in the law for the granting of extra years of credited service, minimum allowances, and limitations on the percentage of final compensation that may be paid for disability retirements.

In brief, every application for a disability retirement is handled as an individual case, on its own merits, in accordance with law.

Death Benefits. *Basic Death Benefit.* The law provides for statutory beneficiaries for the Basic Death Benefit, unless otherwise designated. These beneficiaries are in the following order of priority:

1. Your spouse (wife or husband).
2. Your children (share and share alike).
3. Your parents (share and share alike).
4. Your estate.

If you wish to name different beneficiaries, or list them in a different order of priority, you must fill out a State Form 241, which your employer has. If you file such a form, and your personal circumstances change (through marriage, remarriage, the birth or death of children, divorce, or other personal event) you should fill out a new State Form 241.

The basic death benefit is payable to the beneficiary of active members who die before retiring. The benefit consists of the member's contributions and interest plus an employer furnished benefit equal to one month's salary for each year of service credited, to a maximum of six years of service.

1957 Survivor's Benefit. If, at the time of your death, you had reached 55 years of age, and had five or more years of service, your widow may elect to take the 1957 Survivor's Benefit in lieu of the basic death benefit. The 1957 benefit is payable as a monthly allowance to the surviving widow (or dependent widower) or to children until they reach 18. The amount of the 1957 benefit is one-half of the unmodified allowance, computed as if you had retired on the date of your death.

1959 Survivor's Benefit. This benefit is optional for each employer. Employees working as of the effective date of the exercise of the option by the employer will be given the choice of being covered under this benefit or not; those hired after that date will automatically be covered by the 1959 Survivor's Benefit. The benefit is available only to those NOT covered by Social Security. Members covered by Social Security have similar survivorship protection through the federal program. A premium of $2.00 per month is charged directly to the member. Benefits payable under the 1959 Survivor's Benefits are payable only for death while in an employment status before retiring. Current benefits are:

To an eligible surviving widow (or dependent widower) until remarriage with two or more eligible children; or three eligible children only .... $250 monthly

To an eligible surviving widow (or dependent widower) with one eligible child; or two eligible children only .... $180 monthly

To a surviving widow at age 62 (or dependent widower at age 65), until remarriage; or one eligible child only .... $ 90 monthly

Dependent parents may also be eligible.

This benefit is payable in addition to the 1957 Survivor Benefit or the basic death benefit, as the case may be.

Retired Death Benefit. At the death of a retired member, a $500 death benefit is paid in a lump sum to his statutory or designated beneficiary. The lump sum payment is in addition to any benefit under any optional settlement the member may have selected at retirement.

Service Credit. Prior to 1961 employees were required to serve six months before becoming members of the System. You have the right to receive credit for this "pre-membership" service by making the necessary contributions to the System. Other types of service or absences which you may receive credit for are:

Absence on military service.

Time during which you were absent from service without salary, because of injury or illness arising out of and in the course of your employment and during which time temporary disability payments were received.

Time spent in "public service." Such service includes a wide variety of situations involving the federal government, the university, some nonfederal public agencies, the judicial system, war relocation leave, and others. The exact details and restrictions pertinent to each kind of leave for which the employee may elect to purchase service credit vary. Full details pertinent to a particular case may be obtained from PERS Retirement Officers or the headquarters of the System.

Reinstatement after Retirement. After you have retired and are receiving an allowance from the System, you may not be employed by the State of California, the University, or any public agency under contract with the Public Employees' Retirement System unless you are first reinstated from retirement. There are, however, limited exceptions to this rule. Your employer can advise you regarding these exceptions.

You may return to a contracting public agency (or State) employment if you have been on a voluntary service retirement for at least a year. You must first make application to the Retirement System for reinstatement from retirement. If you meet health, age, and other requirements for reinstatement and return to employment, your retirement allowance will cease. When you again retire, your allowance will include credit for both your earlier service and your service after reinstatement.

APPLYING FOR BENEFITS

Retirement Allowance. Submit your Application for Retirement to the Public Employees' Retirement System about 90 days in advance of your intended retirement. This is done on Retirement Form 369 which your employer will have. Remember that normally your retirement cannot be effective earlier than the first of the month in which your application is received by the System. If you want computations of optional settlements 2 and 3, the name, birth date, and sex of your intended beneficiary must be shown on the application.

The System will advise you of the allowance payable and will furnish the necessary forms and instructions for your retirement.

Death Benefit. Notice of the death of an active member is usually sent to the Retirement System by the employer, or of a retired member by letter from relatives, friends, or other person concerned.

The Retirement System will send an affidavit to the beneficiary for signature with a request for a certified copy of the death certificate. In certain cases, birth or marriage certificates may be required to establish eligibility for survivor benefits.

Refund *(Withdrawal)* of Contributions. As explained above if you have five or more years of credited service at the time you separate from employment, you have the right to elect to leave the accumulated contributions on deposit and apply for an allowance when you reach retirement age. If you elect to have your contributions refunded, you must fill out a form that authorizes the PERS to release the money and submit the completed document through your employer. The proper form is available at your employer's office.

INDEX